for the Love *of the* Sea II

A cookbook to celebrate the British seafood community and their food

Compiled by award-winning author Jenny Jefferies

For the Love of the Sea II

First edition printed in 2023 in the UK

ISBN: 978-1-910863-62-6

Compiled by: Jenny Jefferies

Edited by: Katie Fisher & Phil Turner

Photography by: Paul Gregory, Geoff Reardon, Clair Irwin, Tom O'Brien, DK Photography & Red Zeppelin

Designed by: Paul Cocker

Sales & PR: Emma Toogood & Lizzy Capps

Contributors: Lis Ellis & Lizzie Morton

Published by Meze Publishing Limited
Unit 1b, 2 Kelham Square
Kelham Riverside
Sheffield S3 8SD
Web: www.mezepublishing.co.uk
Telephone: 0114 275 7709
Email: info@mezepublishing.co.uk

Printed by Bell & Bain Ltd, Glasgow

DEDICATION

This book is dedicated to all the fishermen and women.

ACKNOWLEDGEMENTS

Thank you to Mitch Tonks and all the contributors;
to The Food Teachers Centre; to everyone at Meze Publishing:
Phil Turner, Paul Cocker, Katie Fisher, Emma Toogood,
Lizzy Capps, Lis Ellis and Lizzie Morton;
to all the photographers: Paul Gregory, Geoff Reardon, Clair Irwin,
Tom O'Brien, DK Photography and Red Zeppelin;
to my lovely friends and to my wonderful family:
John, Heidi and Florence xxx

FOREWORD

BY MITCH TONKS

Britain's coastline is a seafood frontier, beyond which lies some of the best seafood in the world.

For centuries we have harvested our oceans and fishing has shaped many of our coastal communities. Today, so much of that seafood is exported to nations whose appreciation of eating seafood goes way beyond ours and whose priorities are first and foremost what is put on the table.

In today's ever-changing world we should be concerned with our food security. The seas around our island could provide us with a rich supply of food that is carefully harvested and farmed; we should have no need to sell it to anyone else.

So, what's stopping us? There's no doubt that some of it is about our priorities and how we value food over entertainment and material things. There is also the fact that we are historically nervous about cooking fish and seafood; we tend to opt for what we know and understand which is why salmon, tuna and prawns are the most common species we eat, even though two of these are not caught or reared in our native waters.

It doesn't take much skill to become a confident fish and seafood cook and this delightful book not only inspires you with wonderful pictures of our coastline and of fishermen and their communities, but also with recipes from real people, like me and you, that do love British fish and seafood.

It is a book that I hope will take you on a journey into this world and the joys it can bring to any table and family. There has never been a more important time to value our fishermen and women on this seafood frontier and celebrate our heritage as Islanders. This book celebrates all of those things and takes you on a seafood odyssey that will help you to enjoy our wonderful British fish and seafood, which is some of the very best in the world.

Happy cooking.

Mitch Tonks

PREFACE

· ·

BY JENNY JEFFERIES

This sequel to For The Love of the Sea is a celebration of the small-scale fisherman and woman alongside the hugely important historic crafts, individuals, businesses, and organisations that complement and support them. For The Love of the Sea II champions sustainability, conservation, food provenance, community, and education: topics that are all very close to my heart.

Sustainability means meeting our own needs without compromising the ability of future generations to meet theirs. In addition to natural resources and environmentalism, we also need social and economic resources to achieve this. The sustainability of our fish and seafood species highly depends upon not only the region but the season in which they are caught. So, what may be sustainable for you in one part of the country at a certain time of year may not be for others elsewhere.

It's important to understand these distinctions when choosing what we buy and consume in the UK. As an island nation with a rich and beautiful coast that offers us a bounty of freshly caught fish and seafood, we should be wholeheartedly supporting our fishermen and women. I would urge everyone reading this book to buy local, to buy seasonally, to buy sustainably, and above all to buy British.

I am incredibly grateful to have enjoyed all my childhood holidays by the sea, mainly in the beautiful Devonshire town of Salcombe, and I still make a regular pilgrimage to this sentimental place with my own family. Introducing them to rockpool exploration, messing about in boats, mackerel fishing, collecting beautiful shells, building sandcastles – with as much concentration and delight as their almost immediate destruction – and tasting new fish and seafood for the first time is really important to me.

Creating fond memories and expanding our palates with the delights of the British coast is a big part of these holidays. I always seek out opportunities to try something new at a restaurant that I wouldn't usually cook or eat at home, staying away from the 'big five' most popular species of fish and seafood: prawns, salmon, tuna, cod and haddock. From old favourites such as bass, scallops, mussels, monkfish, and herring to novelties like squid, octopus, clams, and cockles, there is so much more than I can ever imagine.

My experience alone demonstrates the importance of our restaurants, cafés and seaside shacks dotted throughout British coastal towns and villages. They can become the bridge between our homes and the sea. The fishmonger, I believe, is of equal importance. The knowledge, expertise and heritage of both establishments and family businesses are necessary for a thriving economy and help us to uphold culinary traditions that are entwined with our coastal cultures and seaside stories.

I am even more grateful to the fishermen and women who go out to sea and bring back the food we love, for us to enjoy in the warmth of our homes and local restaurants, or even – if you're lucky enough – direct from the boat on the quay.

I fundamentally believe that where there's an opportunity to earn, there's an opportunity to give, which is why I'm donating 10% of my net profits from the sales of For The Love of the Sea II to The Food Teacher's Centre 'Fish In School Hero' programme.

I very much hope that you enjoy this book; the heartfelt stories and exciting recipes showcase the catch of our contributors at their very best. Please do share your cooking and feedback with me on my Instagram page @jennyljefferies – I hope to see you there!

CONTENTS

· ·

THE FOOD TEACHERS CENTRE

BY LOUISE DAVIES, FOUNDER

"We delivered 100kg of Scottish scallops to 50 schools – reaching 5,000 pupils in the areas of deprivation or with the highest free school meals scores – and two tonnes of fresh Devon mussels to 200 schools for 8,000 pupils."

Our 'Fish in School Hero' programme seeks to give secondary school pupils a chance to prepare, cook and eat fish, aiming to develop more positive attitudes towards eating fresh fish sourced in the UK. Through providing locally sourced fish and teacher training, the programme overcomes the current obstacles to lesson planning and gives young people an exciting and delicious experience. It is directed particularly at schools in the most deprived areas, where pupils are unlikely to have access to fresh fish and more than 50% had never cooked fresh fish before, even in areas where the fishing industry exists.

More than 900 schools took part in 2021-22, with 13,000 pupils having a unique opportunity to prepare, cook and taste fresh fish. We delivered 100kg of Scottish scallops to 50 schools – reaching 5,000 pupils in the areas of deprivation or with the highest free school meals scores – and two tonnes of fresh Devon mussels to 200 schools for 8,000 pupils. There was no cost to the schools involved, and the pupils learned about provenance, sustainability, seasonality, and how quickly fish can be prepared and cooked for appetising and nutritious meals. The fish was delivered thanks to an exceptional partnership created by the Food Teacher's Centre with Fishmongers' Company's Fisheries Charitable Trust, together with Offshore Shellfish Ltd, MacDuff, M&J Seafood, and Fowey Shellfish Co.

More than 1,027 Food and Nutrition teachers were trained as part of the programme and supported with resources to bring their cooking lessons to life. This included a full teaching pack with a video of the shellfish from harvest to plate, a range of recipes suitable for classrooms and young people, and a school risk assessment. We also provide a teacher training workshop and briefing, online training, a best practice sharing platform, and in some cases industry representatives who talk first-hand about bringing seafood from the sea to the plate, highlighting careers in the fishing industry.

The feedback from pupils (via a FISH 2021-22 survey of 200 participating schools) on the cooking and tasting experience demonstrated a marked change in their confidence and attitudes towards fresh fish. After the programme, 67% said 'I would like to try preparing and cooking fish again' while 69% said that 'the fish masterclass has given me more confidence in preparing and cooking fish'' and 66% said 'I would like to eat more fish in the future'.

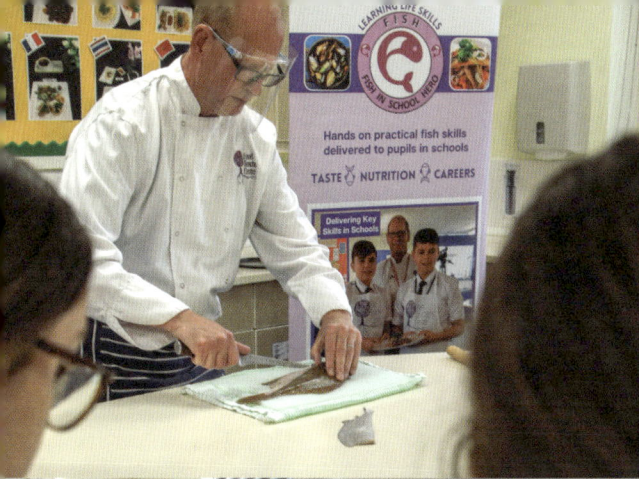

A&J FRESH FISH LTD

BY AMY FARISH

"I have always had boats and am a keen sailor and sea angler; I used to fish four lobster pots from my old boat for leisure. In 2021, we felt it was the right time for us to take the leap and buy our own commercial fishing vessel."

I am a commercial fisherwoman and a co-director of A&J Fresh Fish Ltd. Having been in the fishing industry for a year now at the age of 30, I own a seven metre Colne Catamaran with my boyfriend which we use to fish lobster pots, prawn pots and fixed gill nets. I have always had boats and am a keen sailor and sea angler; I used to fish four lobster pots from my old boat for leisure. In 2021, we felt it was the right time for us to take the leap and buy our own commercial fishing vessel. After pulling together savings and selling our beloved limited edition Land Rover Defender, we bought the Colne Catamaran from Kirkcudbright.

I sadly lost my dad in 2020 and he was one of the main reasons I wanted to give this new venture a go, as he used to take me fishing when I was younger which is where my love of the sea started. The drive behind establishing our business here in Cumbria was that we felt there wasn't anywhere around us that was supplying fresh, local and sustainably caught shellfish and wet fish. We decided that A&J Fresh Fish Ltd – named after us, Amy and Jack – was going to supply the people of Walney Island, Barrow-in-Furness and the surrounding Lake District with the freshest and best quality seafood possible! In order to keep our catch fresh and in the best condition for our customers, we hold shellfish in our specially designed tank which has been a great asset to our business. In the future, we plan on purchasing more tanks to enable us to supply shellfish in greater numbers.

The sea has always been a huge part of my life and I have always had a keen interest in and love for the commercial side of fishing. I am a mechanical fitter by trade, so I was always interested in the hydraulics and the mechanical gear the commercial boats carry. This business is extremely important to me, and I get so much joy out of delivering fresh seafood to our customers. I look forward to my next 20 years and beyond working in the commercial fishing industry.

TRADITIONAL STYLE POTTED CRAB IN BUTTER

This simple but delicious recipe uses fresh brown and white crab meat, potted in butter with herbs and spices: absolutely perfect on toast after a hard day at sea!

1 large cooked brown crab

¼ tsp grated nutmeg

Pinch of cayenne pepper (add as much or as little as you like depending on how spicy you like it)

Salt and pepper

2 lemons, juiced

200g salted butter

Handful of fresh parsley, finely chopped

Remove the brown and white meat from the cooked crab. Gently mix the crab meat with the nutmeg, cayenne pepper, salt, pepper, and lemon juice in a large bowl.

Melt the butter in a saucepan, then pour half of the melted butter into the crab mixture. Stir until well combined.

Spoon the crab and butter mixture into ramekins or small tubs and flatten the top with a spoon to create a level surface.

Pour an equal amount of the remaining melted butter into each ramekin or tub to seal the crab mixture. Sprinkle with the fresh parsley.

Place the potted crab in the fridge for up to an hour until set. Enjoy on some fresh sourdough or toast of your choice.

ANDY CHADWICK

EEL FISHERMAN ON THE EXE ESTUARY, DEVON

"Historically, most eels caught in the UK ended up on the London or Dutch markets with various agents travelling the length and breadth of the country to collect this once very lucrative bounty."

It all started for me at a very young age, following in the footsteps of my father. At just 12 I was a fully paid-up member of his crew working after school hours and during the holidays. Mostly it was salmon netting with some grey mullet, bass, herring and eel netting thrown in. Now that fishing for salmon, mullet and all species other than eels is forbidden on all English estuaries – and because I'm passionate about keeping age old traditions alive – it's the latter that I now concentrate my efforts on. The method I use is the Fyke net, a Dutch invention that has been used in the UK on many waterways, including the Exe, for well over a century.

Historically, most eels caught in the UK ended up on the London or Dutch markets with various agents travelling the length and breadth of the country to collect this once very lucrative bounty. However, with stocks reportedly at an all-time low, strict regulations are now in place and rightly so, as the eel does need some protection. This has also resulted in fishing efforts being at an all-time low though, and the travelling agents are now redundant as there is simply not enough fish on the market to make it worth their while.

For a short while, I sent my catch via courier to London for the local traditional jellying market, but it was a time consuming and expensive way of doing things and frankly unviable. If I was to continue, my only option was to market the product locally myself… Due to their slippery, slimy, snake-like appearance eels are most definitely not to every fish eater's liking, especially for those residing well away from the metropolis, so marketing my catch in deepest Devon was never going to be easy. However, following a conversation with a local fishmonger and smokehouse owner it was concluded that hot smoking the eel over oak chips to make it more appealing was the way forward.

This proved to be absolutely the right approach and by dealing with a local restaurant, a few private clients and attending the occasional street market each year, I have no problem selling my very modest catch, ninety percent of which is hot smoked. As much as I love smoked eel myself, the recipe I have shared for this book is by far my favourite way of eating eel: very simple yet delicious and something I hope you can enjoy trying too.

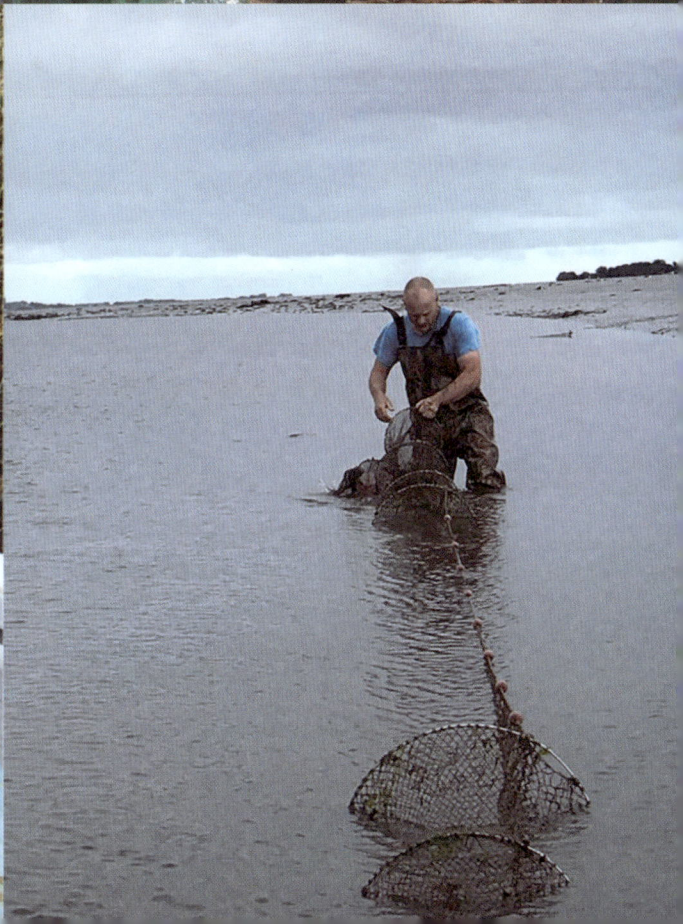

PAN-FRIED EEL

I was given this recipe many years ago by an Italian friend, chef and restaurant owner who I once supplied, sadly no longer with us. It was served as a starter in his restaurant, and I am told it's a traditional Christmas meal in Italy.

1 clove of garlic

500g whole skinned eel, cut into 8 chunks

Sprinkle of coarse sea salt

Sprinkle of black pepper

1 tbsp extra virgin olive oil

2 tbsp white wine vinegar

Plain flour, for coating

Vegetable oil, for frying

1 fresh lemon

Crusty bread

Butter

Peel and crush or cut the garlic clove in half and rub the cut sides over each piece of eel, aiming to cover the whole surface area.

Place the eel chunks in a small dish, season with salt and pepper, drizzle with the olive oil and vinegar, then leave to marinate in the fridge for 1 hour.

Remove the fish from the marinade and coat with the flour, shaking off any excess. Preheat the vegetable oil in a pan until bubbling hot and then fry the eel chunks, turning occasionally, until they are crisp and golden brown.

Drain the excess oil by placing the fried eel on kitchen towel and then serve with plenty of lemon wedges and buttered crusty bread.

PREPARATION TIME: I HOUR I5 MINUTES | COOKING TIME: I5 MINUTES | SERVES 4 AS A STARTER OR 2 AS A MAIN

BARNEYS BILLINGSGATE LTD.

BY MARK BUTTON

"There's so much fantastic seafood in our waters and we shouldn't be afraid to try new things. Quality products like ours can be great value, quick and easy to cook, sustainable and delicious: you can't go wrong."

In early 1969 Eddie Button, my father, started a wholesale jellied eel and shellfish business in a very small shop on Old Montague Street in East London. He built a successful business supplying shellfish stalls in East London and later purchased a wholesale business from one of his customers, Barney Gritzman. Eddie decided to keep the name and Barneys Seafood operated from the premises on Chamber Street until October 2019. I joined the business in the early 1980s, learning all aspects of the business from my father, and became managing director after Eddie passed away in 2008.

The business today is very different to the one my father started all those years ago. People's tastes have changed, a far greater range of products is now available, and people are far more health conscious. Having said all of this, the principles of running a successful fish and shellfish business are still the same; work starts at 4am come rain or shine, preparing eels is still a hard, time consuming and extremely skilled business, the customer is always right (well, mostly) and quality is everything.

Since October 2019, Barneys has been fully based at Billingsgate Fish Market with a shop and factory unit. We still specialise in providing the finest jellied eels and shellfish, just as we have done for 50 years, but have also added many new product lines, from snow crab claws to lobster tails, and now sell over 250 different types of fish and seafood. My father started with just seven! We source eels from England and Ireland throughout the summer season, as well as local products including cockles from Leigh-on-Sea, whelks from the South Coast and oysters from Maldon and Mersey.

My sons have since joined me and between us we work every night and day of the week, providing customers with a service that I think is second to none. They know we offer a personal touch that my years of experience and the knowledge passed down from my father adds to our business. I enjoy seeing this industry develop and want to help other businesses develop and thrive alongside ours. There's so much fantastic seafood in our waters and we shouldn't be afraid to try new things. Quality products like ours can be great value, quick and easy to cook, sustainable and delicious: you can't go wrong.

BILLINGSGATE MARKET

Serving the
Finest
Jellied Eels
fish & Seafood
over 50 years

BARNEYS SEAFOOD
020 7481 2177 www.barneys-seafood.co.uk

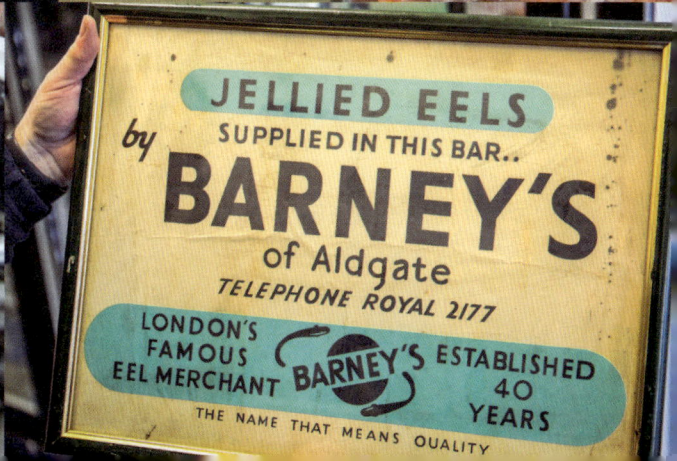

JELLIED EELS
by SUPPLIED IN THIS BAR..
BARNEY'S
of Aldgate
TELEPHONE ROYAL 2177
LONDON'S
FAMOUS BARNEY'S ESTABLISHED
EEL MERCHANT 40 YEARS
THE NAME THAT MEANS QUALITY

STEWED OR JELLIED EELS

· ·

This recipe allows you to prepare one of my favourite seafoods in two different ways.
Not everyone loves the traditional jellied eels, but they couldn't be simpler to make.

700g (1 ½ lbs) eels

Salt and pepper

1 tbsp malt vinegar

1 tbsp pimentos

A few springs of parsley

1 bay leaf

1 tbsp lemon juice

1 tsp gelatine (for jellied eels)

Ask your fishmonger to prepare the eels, or to do this yourself, cut off the head and cut the eels into 5cm (2 inch) pieces.

Put the eel pieces into a large saucepan and add 275ml (half a pint) of cold water along with the vinegar, pimentos, parsley and bay leaf. Season with salt and pepper to taste.

Bring the contents of your pan to the boil, then simmer for about 25 minutes or until the eel is tender. Remove the parsley sprigs, bay leaf and pimentos.

Stir the lemon juice into the stew, then pour the eels and broth into bowls to serve.

To make jellied eels, follow exactly the same method but stir in the gelatine while the stew is cooking. Once done, leave to cool and then refrigerate for at least 4 hours. When thoroughly chilled, the stock forms a soft edible jelly around the eels.

COASTAL FORAGING

BY CRAIG EVANS

"I've had a lifelong passion for foraging since the age of six or seven, when my dad used to take me and my brothers cockle picking."

I take groups of people from all over the world on coastal foraging expeditions in an area of Wales which covers about 150 miles, from Carmarthenshire to most of Pembrokeshire. The coastline here is so diverse, with sand dune systems, rivers, estuaries, sandy beaches, rocky headlands… not forgetting the Bristol Channel which has the second highest tidal range in the world. Because the beaches tend to have shallow shelving, even a small difference in the height of the tide leaves a lot more of the shore exposed, meaning we can access everything that there is to find.

There are about a dozen different types of seaweed you can forage here, including the delicious pepper dulce or 'sea truffle' which tastes of butter, wild garlic, and – believe it or not – truffle. We get a dozen or so different species of shellfish, crustaceans including lobsters and four or five species of crab, then of course all kinds of fish. It's very easy to knock up a meal sustainably and you can even eat some things raw, like certain types of seaweed and razor clam feet. At the end of every course, we cook whatever we find in a simple but delicious one pot meal that might feature edible shoreline plants such as samphire or sea radish alongside the foraged shellfish.

I've had a lifelong passion for foraging since the age of six or seven, when my dad used to take me and my brothers cockle picking. What I do isn't just about foraging and food though; I have a huge drive to educate people, so I also teach at local colleges, offer free school visits and do talks at various events. For me, this education encompasses everything to do with the shore: geology, history, biodiversity, even sustainable tourism and hospitality. I've been fortunate enough to develop quite a reach through my YouTube channel and appearances on TV programmes with the likes of Mary Berry, Michael Portillo, Grace Dent and even Ainsley Harriott! Although I never planned for this to be so successful, I'm proud to have created a thriving business over the last five years.

The tricky part is that if we encouraged everyone to go foraging, there wouldn't be any coastal plants and animals left! So, as much as I want to share my passion for it, there's also an important element of balance to consider. I'm involved in a local seaweed and shellfish farm which produces wonderful coastal food in a sustainable manner, and I strongly believe that we should all be finding ways to look after the environment around our shores while enjoying them too.

WILD FORAGED SEAFOOD ONE POT WONDER

. . . .

I've developed this really easy recipe using some the finds we encounter on my coastal foraging courses. The only ingredient I bring along is unsalted Sir Gar Carmarthenshire butter, made a mile from my home, and the rest of the suggestions below will depend on what your coastline offers!

200g unsalted butter

Wild garlic bulbs

Edible flowers

Rosehips

Rock samphire

Pepper dulse

Dulse seaweed

Cockles

Mussels

Soft shell or gaper clams

Razor clams

Prawns

Brown shrimp

Velvet swimming crab

Brown crab

Lobster

We normally come across wild garlic bulbs and leaves, edible flowers, rosehips, rock samphire, pepper dulse and dulse seaweed, very large cockles, mussels, soft shell or gaper clams, razor clams (depending on the tide level), prawns, brown shrimp, velvet swimming and brown crabs, and the very occasional lobster depending on season. Very rarely we find octopus, but we don't eat these.

Wash all the sand off the clams and debeard the mussels, then wash the seaweeds. Chop up the wild garlic bulbs, rock samphire, pepper dulse and dulse seaweed.

Melt the butter in a saucepan or wok, then stir fry the prepared ingredients above until the flavours are mixed in with the butter. Take care not to burn the butter at this stage.

Add the foraged seafood to the pan, then place some rock samphire and edible flowers and/or rosehips on top. Add a small amount of fresh water to start the steaming process and cover with a lid.

Steam for around 8 minutes or so to allow all the seafood juices to mix with the stir-fried ingredients.

Once all the seafood is cooked and the shells have opened, serve in bowls with some of the delicious juices poured over the seafood.

PREPARATION TIME: 15 MINUTES | COOKING TIME: 15 MINUTES | SERVES HOWEVER MANY ARE IN YOUR FORAGING PARTY

CORNISH SEA SALT

BY PHILIP TANSWELL, MANAGING DIRECTOR

"Drawn from the unique properties of Cornwall's clear ocean waters, which provide Cornish Sea Salt with its elevated and unique taste profile, the diverse range of sea salts are hand-harvested to deliver maximum flavour."

Cornish Sea Salt is harvested fresh from the sea, just eight metres from its eco-friendly salt house on the Lizard Peninsula, Cornwall. Founded in 2007 from humble beginnings on the south Cornish coast, our signature blue pots sit just as happily in Michelin-starred establishments as they do on the tables of home cooks, who have an appreciation not only for the taste and quality of artisan sea salt, but the exciting versatility and creativity it can bring to cooking.

Drawn from the unique properties of Cornwall's clear ocean waters, which provide Cornish Sea Salt with its elevated and unique taste profile, the diverse range of sea salts are hand-harvested to deliver maximum flavour. They contain over 60 naturally occurring minerals as well as being naturally lower in sodium than table salt. These Grade A waters possess a distinct mineral profile thanks to the area's unusual rock geology.

At Cornish Sea Salt, we are passionate about food but are all about keeping things simple. Salt is the carrier of flavour, and we like to describe our sea salt as the amplifier, giving zing and zest to dishes. Where ingredients come from is also extremely important to us, especially when it comes to fish. As mentioned, our sea salt is harvested from Grade A waters which means you can eat the fish fresh from the sea as it is so clean. You can see a mussel farm from our salt house in the ocean which produces some of the most delicious mussels we've eaten.

From our core range of crunchy sea salt crystals and soft finishing flakes to the ever-evolving blended seasonings and the deep umami tastes of our seaweed salts, Cornish Sea Salt can suit the everyday amateur as well as the seasoned chef. Our products are available in the UK at Sainsburys, Waitrose, Tesco, Asda, Morrisons and The Co-Op, as well as internationally in over 35 countries.

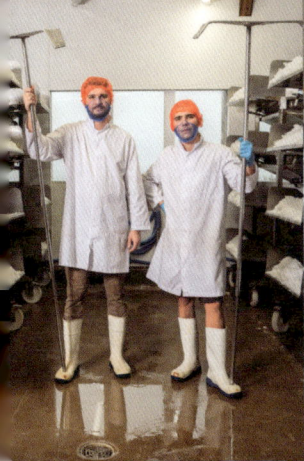

GRILLED MACKEREL WITH BEETROOT, APPLE AND FENNEL SALAD

....

This is a celebration of wintery flavours that marry beautifully with the popular Cornish fish, served with creamed horseradish and tarragon oil. It may look fancy but is very easy to execute and makes a great starter for a dinner party or a light lunch.

2 whole mackerel, butterflied (or 4 fillets)

3 raw or cooked beetroot

2 eating apples (I used Granny Smiths but any variety is fine)

1 small fennel bulb

2 lemons, juiced

5 tbsp extra virgin olive oil

Black pepper, to taste

Cornish Sea Salt Flakes

5-6 sprigs of tarragon

1 clove of garlic, finely chopped

Cornish Sea Salt & Peppery Blend

4 tbsp horseradish

6 tbsp creme fraiche

1 tbsp groundnut or veg oil

To butterfly the mackerel, cut the head off and then cut all the way along from the belly to the tail.

Remove the spine (the easiest way to do this is using scissors) and as many pin bones as possible. Alternatively, ask your fishmonger to butterfly them for you.

Now prepare the salad. If you have raw beetroot, roast or boil them whole before removing the skin, which comes off easily once cooked, and cutting into wedges. Prepare the apples by coring and cutting into cubes. Cut the fennel bulb in half and then thinly slice lengthways, preferably using a mandoline, reserving any bright green fronds from the top.

Toss the beetroot, apples and fennel in half the lemon juice and a little olive oil. Season to taste with some cracked black pepper and Cornish Sea Salt Flakes.

Strip the leaves off the tarragon sprigs and chop them finely along with any fennel fronds. Mix these into the remaining lemon juice and olive oil along with the garlic. Season with a pinch of Cornish Sea Salt & Peppery Blend to taste.

In a separate bowl, mix the horseradish and creme fraiche together, then season with a pinch of Cornish Sea Salt Flakes and cracked black pepper.

Once you have prepared the salad, tarragon oil and creamed horseradish, whack your grill to the highest setting and place the mackerel skin side up on a tray, making sure you butterfly it out. Brush the skin with the groundnut or vegetable oil and season generously with Cornish Sea Salt Flakes. Mackerel cooks very quickly so after a maximum of 5-8 minutes under the grill, the skin should start blistering while the underneath steams. Do not turn the mackerel over.

Once the mackerel is ready, assemble your dish by placing your salad onto the plate. Add the mackerel, dot the creamed horseradish around the plate and then drizzle over the tarragon oil.

PREPARATION TIME: 20 MINUTES | COOKING TIME: 15 MINUTES | SERVES 2

CRABPOTCELLARS

BY SUSAN MORGAN

"I teach pot making as a two-day course from home and at our fishing store down the road. My trade name, Crabpotcellars, comes from the traditional name for a fisherman's store in the village, called cellars."

My husband David and I live in the fishing village of Hope Cove. He is the last full-time fisher living in Hope, while I make the traditional style willow or withy pots for catching crab and lobster. I always enjoyed arts and crafts as well as biological sciences, and my former partner was keen on crab and lobster fishing in his spare time from his holiday home in South Devon. When we moved to Devon permanently having bought a house in Hope in 1985, I began learning about making withy pots from a local fisher, Eric Jarvis. At this time, crab was still being transported from Hope Cove harbour beach, so fishing had a strong community presence.

Sadly, when Eric died in 1992 I only had a few photographs of the method for making the withy pots. However, I persevered and researched archive photos of local potmakers, soon realising there were both regional and personal differences in techniques. This research also gave me an understanding of how rapidly the old style fishery, using 80-100 pots for two men in an open boat, had transformed to one using up to 300 pots per man, on an inshore boat.

I joined the Basketmakers Association to broaden my skill base and met David around that time on the beach in Hope. After we married, I threw myself into pot making which provided an additional income to my main work as a primary school teacher. Along with another basket maker, Hilary Burns, I acquired a willow platt to grow the materials for making withy pots, and until recently had an allotment where I grew various colours of willow.

I now teach pot making as a two-day course from home and at our fishing store down the road. My trade name, Crabpotcellars, comes from the traditional name for a fisherman's store in the village, called cellars. Tourists are the main customers who buy the pots – some to fish with, some for decoration – though I have also supplied film and stage sets. I am passionate about teaching craft skills and their relationship to environmental awareness, so I aim to continue this and my research into our local village history. David and I eat a lot of fish, mostly simple shellfish preparations but occasionally other favourites including bisques, quiches and crab cakes. We have presented shellfish picking demonstrations and withy pot making at local events as well as regularly supplying our local customers with crab and lobster.

LOBSTER LINGUINE

· ·

This recipe originated to use up leftover lobster or crab from a seafood salad meal for guests, David having brought in more than we needed from the boat. This recipe succeeds either by 'stretching' small amounts of shellfish or being rather more generous depending on what you have to hand.

1 lobster, cooked and picked (15 minutes boiling for 750g, 20 minutes for 1kg)

500g fresh or dried linguine or tagliatelle

1 tbsp olive oil

Knob of butter

1 onion, finely chopped

1-2 spring onions, thinly sliced

1 clove of garlic, or to taste

1 medium heat chilli, deseeded and finely chopped (optional)

1 tin of chopped tomatoes, or the equivalent amount of fresh, fleshy tomatoes, roughly chopped

2 tbsp dry vermouth, wine or brandy

100ml fish stock (optional)

100ml cream

Fresh basil, chopped (leave some leaves whole for garnish)

Salt and pepper

Dice the picked lobster meat and set aside. The coral or eggs are good in this dish because of their bright red colour.

If your pasta is dried, get a pan of salted water boiling and drop in the linguine or tagliatelle to cook for 10 minutes.

Meanwhile, start the sauce by heating the oil and butter. Fry the onions and garlic until softened but not browned, then add the chilli, tomatoes and vermouth.

Simmer the sauce for 10 minutes, adding the fish stock if desired for a looser consistency. Once simmered, stir in the cooked lobster for just long enough to heat through – do not overcook it.

If you are using fresh pasta, drop it into a pan of boiling salted water now to cook for 2 minutes. Add the cream and basil to the lobster sauce, then season with salt and black pepper to taste.

Pour the finished lobster sauce over the drained pasta in bowls or toss them together before serving. Garnish with the reserved basil leaves and enjoy.

PREPARATION TIME: 15 MINUTES | COOKING TIME: 15 MINUTES | 1 X 750G LOBSTER WILL SERVE 2-3 PEOPLE (1KG SERVES 4)

DAN THE FISH MAN

"My watchword has always been Healthy Fish, Healthy Heart, and I'm intensely proud of the fish I buy and sell. Almost all of it is landed fresh at Appledore Dock by local fishermen plying the seas around our North Devon coasts."

I've been involved in fishing and the sea for as long as I can remember. For forty-two years I've been lucky enough to live in Clovelly, the unique and beautiful North Devon village with a rich fishing heritage going back centuries. I spent many years drifting for herring in the waters off Lundy, following in the footsteps of hardy Clovelly fishermen down the ages. I found selling the fruits of my catches just as fascinating. Now I encourage my customers to experience the very best in fish and seafood cooking – we are especially lucky here in North Devon to fish in the cleanest seas in Britain.

My watchword has always been Healthy Fish, Healthy Heart, and I'm intensely proud of the fish I buy and sell. Almost all of it is landed fresh at Appledore Dock by local fishermen plying the seas around our North Devon coasts. My enthusiasm soon turned into a crusade, and I set up the first fishermen's collective at Clovelly. This proved successful and made me realise how lucky we are to enjoy the bounty we receive from the seas here in North Devon. I began taking my barrow to local markets, where I encouraged customers to be as enthusiastic about fish cuisine as I am.

I'm immensely proud to have been a lifeboatman at Clovelly for many years. Helping people in distress in the hazardous waters around our Devon coasts is a moving experience, and it has deepened my sense of social responsibility. I take from the sea, and I believe it's equally important to give something back. So, I love visiting schools where I work with children, cooking up simple recipes with healthy local produce that doesn't come in plastic supermarket packets. I also donate a quantity of fish weekly to a local food bank.

The joy of fish cuisine is that it doesn't have to be complicated. Over the years at local markets, I've enjoyed chatting with customers, sharing and exchanging ideas. As a result, I've developed a style of simple recipes that I believe make the most of our superb local fish and seafood. Cooking and eating in the open air is particularly exhilarating, and each year I visit Lundy island where I cook up mouth-watering dishes on the beach: there's nothing like it!

Meanwhile, the fish fight goes on! I'd like to thank all my customers old and new for sharing my passion for fish, and I look forward to seeing you again soon.

NAUGHTY KIPPERS

For a slow weekend or cosy morning, try indulging yourself and a friend with this combination.

1 large natural kipper

1 dessert spoon thick-cut English marmalade

1 full glass of very chilled white Rioja or Spanish sanlucca

Steep the kipper in very hot water for 8 minutes.

Serve on a warm plate with the spoonful of the marmalade and plenty of your favourite toasted bread.

Dan's Tips:

I think it is essential to start with tasting the smoked fish and follow that with sips of white wine. A great start to the day if you're not driving!

PREPARATION TIME: 5 MINUTES | COOKING TIME: 10 MINUTES | SERVES 2

DAVID HUGHES
DAI'S SHED

· ·

BY GILL BAILEY

"We would like to see the British people making more of the high quality seafood found in our waters and being more adventurous in the species they try."

Dai's hometown of Aberdyfi has a small fishing fleet; now only three boats fish out of the harbour regularly. He was born in the village, where we continue to live and work, and has been fishing for fish and shellfish – now mainly prawns, brown crab and lobster – for many years. He works around a hundred pots in Cardigan Bay single-handedly, though there are larger boats with many more pots working in the area.

Eight years ago, with the help of grants, we opened a small processing unit and shop on the wharf named Dai's Shed, where all of Dai's catch of brown crab are dressed and sold by us locally. Much of the lobster too is sold from the shop, either live or dressed, and both prove very popular with locals and tourists alike. Selling to the public gives him time to enjoy interacting with customers and adds variety to his working week.

Dai begins the season fishing for prawns which are mainly sold abroad but year on year, probably down to overfishing, the crab and lobster on the inside ground (and to some extent mackerel) have declined. Because of this he has been targeting whelks, which are growing in popularity, and some of the many spider crab that now move into our waters during the warmer months. He is hoping to begin processing the spider crab for the local market with the aim of filling in for the loss of our very popular dressed brown crab. We would like to see the British people making more of the high quality seafood found in our waters and being more adventurous in the species they try.

Fishing as a profession is demanding on your time and energy. It takes courage and a willingness to work long, often unsociable, hours, not only on the fishing side but on maintaining the pots, nets and the boat, plus the ever-changing paperwork. It is extremely important to maintain and grow the stocks for future generations and we wish the Welsh Government would consider improving regulations, such as insisting on the addition of escape hatches on lobster pots and not allowing the landing of berried lobsters to help stop the decline and ensure an improved fishery, as they have done in other countries. Dai is nearing retirement and as obtaining crew members has always been a problem in this industry, we have no plans to expand the business, but hope we can continue to make a living from the sea for as long as possible.

STEAMED GREY MULLET WITH
SPRING ONIONS, GARLIC AND GINGER

I have heard that this fish is thought to have a muddy flavour, but Dai catches grey mullet in the estuary and it really is a delicious meaty fish, often also enjoyed by the local ospreys. This is the recipe that we suggest to customers, and they usually come back for more.

1 whole grey mullet, scaled and gutted

2 spring onions, sliced diagonally

2 cloves of garlic, sliced thinly

1 thumb sized piece of fresh ginger, sliced thinly

Olive oil

A little lemon juice (optional)

Salt and pepper to taste

Preheat your oven to 200°c. Take your scaled and gutted whole mullet (we leave the head and tail on for flavour, but you can remove it if preferred) and score three or more diagonal slashes on either side. If you can't get grey mullet, bream would be a good alternative.

Stuff the spring onion, garlic and ginger into the flesh. Oil a large piece of tin foil and place the fish in the centre.

Sprinkle with salt and ground black pepper to taste, then squeeze over a little lemon juice too if you like. Wrap the fish loosely and seal the foil tightly to form a package.

Place the foil package on a shallow tray and bake in the preheated oven for around 25-30 minutes. We enjoy this simply with boiled potatoes, peas and a little cheese sauce.

DAVID MORGAN

· ·

CRAB AND LOBSTER FISHERMAN, SOUTH DEVON

"I pride myself on the way I maintain my boat and equipment, as well as selecting and handling the catch. I also take a strong interest in the sustainability and protective management of the local fishing industry."

I was brought up on a farm just two miles from the beach at Hope but with no history of fishing in the family; life was based around the farm. As a teenager my two passions were sport – mainly rugby – and then fishing, which developed from going to the beach at Hope with other lads from my school and watching the fishers catching crab and lobster off Bolt Tail or netting across Bigbury Bay. At the time, there was a community of fishers in Hope harbour with small boats manned by one or two people and inkwell crabpots. These were initially made with withies but over the years transitioned to wire and then plastic as things shifted towards a more modern fishery.

One of these fishers, Eric Jarvis, became my mentor and would take myself and a friend to sea throughout my teenage years. When I declared to my parents that I wanted to fish, they were adamant that I should get higher level qualifications first. So I went into the Merchant Navy as an apprentice deck officer and came out ten years later as a navigation officer after travelling the world and having various spells in college to gain my OND. Every leave period I was back on the beach fishing and making plans to buy my own boat, along with three or four other young men who also bought boats at about the same time. These were dories, suitable for single handed cove fishing and small enough to need removing from the beach during storms. I now have a 10 metre boat, kept at Salcombe for the harbour and boat servicing facilities, but am still fishing those same grounds.

When I started out, the crabs were collected and packed live from the beach at Hope Cove, for shipment mostly to France and Spain. Nowadays crabs are collected direct from Salcombe; only live crab and lobster is saleable and must be handled and packed carefully. I pride myself on the way I maintain my boat and equipment, as well as selecting and handling the catch. I also take a strong interest in the sustainability and protective management of the local fishing industry. As such, I am chairman of the South Devon and Channel Shellfishermen Ltd, an association of fishers, gear suppliers and merchants that seeks to enhance and protect the local fishery. I am also a marine management appointee to the Devon and Severn Inshore Fisheries and Conservation Authority (IFCA).

BASS EN PAPILLOTE

This cooking method works wonderfully to produce juicy and aromatic fish dishes, presenting whole fish such as bass, sea bream or mullet in an attractive way using a greaseproof paper or foil envelope. The herbs and other flavourings can easily be adapted to suit your preferences.

1 whole bass, gutted and cleaned

Butter or olive oil

Salt and pepper

1-2 onions, sliced

1 fennel bulb, thinly sliced (or you can use sprigs of dill instead)

1 lemon, cut into slices or wedges

Sprigs of fresh thyme

A dry wine

Note that a 42cm wild-caught bass will feed 2-3 people but farmed fish may be smaller. If you are using red mullet, serve this as individual parcels with one fish per person.

Brush a large piece of greaseproof paper or tin foil generously with the butter or olive oil. Season your cleaned fish with salt and pepper inside and out. Score the sides of larger fish.

Place the fish on the greased paper or foil and fill the cavity with onions, fennel or dill, a couple of lemon slices and some thyme. Add another knob of butter to the cavity with a splash of wine.

Fold the paper or foil over the fish and crimp to seal in all the juices. Place the whole parcel on a baking tray and cook in a preheated oven at 220°c for 10-15 minutes.

Check the parcel after 10 minutes; the fish is ready when it just pulls away from the bone. A large single bass may take 20 minutes.

Serve your bass en papillote with new potatoes and a tomato or green salad.

PREPARATION TIME: 20-30 MINUTES | COOKING TIME: 10-20 MINUTES | SERVES 2-3 (SEE METHOD)

DORSET SHELLFISH

BY CAROLINE DREVER

"We cook and handpick all the crab meat we use, which of course is wild and local. We really do know where it's come from, as the products only travel about eight miles from the crab pots to our production kitchen on Portland."

My partner Graham has been a fisherman since he was a schoolboy, following in his father's footsteps. Graham fishes out of Weymouth for crab, lobster and line-caught fish such as sea bass. Our son has worked with him for the last 14 years and we have two commercial fishing boats in Weymouth.

I decided to leave my job with the local council and sell their catch direct to the public. For me, promoting local fish and encouraging people to eat more seafood was important, and I was able to use Graham's crab, lobster and fish as it was right on tap. Of course, being fishing it is weather and tide dependant, but we are able to fish all year round (most of the time)!

That was 12 years ago. I started to trade with Dorset Farmers' Markets at various towns around Dorset and Somerset and also at food festivals. It soon became clear that people wanted more products and ready meals, so when our daughter Stef started working for me we soon developed various recipes. We now make fish pies, red Thai crab soup, crab pâté, crab linguine, various fish cakes and crab cakes. We also sell our lovely dressed crabs, crab meat, and cooked and dressed lobsters.

We have won various awards over the years, including Great Taste awards for the dressed crab, crab cakes, crab pâté and crab meat as well as Taste of the West Awards for our red Thai crab soup and crab cakes. We have also won awards from Taste of Dorset and Dorset Food and Drink.

We cook and handpick all the crab meat we use, which of course is wild and local. We really do know where it's come from, as the products only travel about eight miles from the crab pots to our production kitchen on Portland.

We really do enjoy catching and selling our products direct to the public; having someone tell you they enjoyed your food makes it all worthwhile. We continue to look at creating more recipes and are always happy to offer guidance on cooking fish, as we love eating and cooking it too! We are very fortunate to have such a great family business and hope it continues long into the future.

DORSET
SHELLFISH

FRESH FISH
& SHELLFISH

We are
OPEN

CRAB
MEAT

DORSET
SHELLFISH

RAB
MEAT

CRAB
MEAT

DORSET
SHELLFISH

CRAB CAKES

· ·

This recipe uses only white crab meat, with no potatoes or breadcrumbs to bulk it out: indulgent but worth it! We make these using our own fresh handpicked white crab meat. These crab cakes are perfect for a light supper or starter.

200g handpicked white crab meat

3 tsp mayonnaise

2 tsp chopped parsley

1 tsp lemon juice

Salt and pepper, to taste

2 tbsp plain flour

1 egg

1 tbsp milk

6 tbsp panko breadcrumbs

Cooking oil, to shallow fry

Combine the crab meat, mayonnaise, parsley, lemon juice and seasoning in a mixing bowl. Mix with a fork or your fingertips. Divide the mixture into 4 equal portions and shape into little patties or flattened balls on a chopping board. You may need a little flour on your hands to do this.

Place the crab cakes in the fridge for about 15 minutes to firm up a little, or they can be left covered overnight in the fridge at this stage.

Whisk the egg and milk together in a shallow bowl. Remove the crab cakes from the fridge and coat them in the remaining flour. Using a fork, lower them into the egg mixture and coat, then place into the panko breadcrumbs and cover completely. Don't worry if they look a little misshapen, as you can reshape them before cooking.

If you have a deep fat fryer, heat the oil to 160°c. If you are shallow frying the crab cakes, have at least 4cm of oil in a frying pan on a medium-hot heat. It's ready when a few breadcrumbs sizzle in the oil.

Fry the crab cakes for at least 2 minutes and 30 seconds in the deep fat fryer, turning as they cook to get a good golden colour with a crisp crumb all over. They may need slightly longer in a frying pan.

Drain the crab cakes on kitchen paper to remove excess oil, then serve with green salad and new potatoes with aioli or a chilli jam dip.

PREPARATION TIME: 30 MINUTES | COOKING TIME: 5 MINUTES | SERVES 2-4

EWING SEAFOODS

···

BY CRAWFORD EWING

"We focused on quality and service for the personal touch and are now supplying all northern Ireland's top hotels and restaurants with fresh seafood daily."

I am a managing director at our family business which has been trading for over 100 years. Ewing Seafoods was established in 1911 by my grandfather Mathew Ewing. He started with a single shop in the heart of Belfast, on Shankill Road, which quickly grew to six shops dotted around the greater Belfast area. Back then, business in Belfast was bustling with the Titanic docks and ship building industry which was the big employer in the day. Ewing Seafoods were fortunate enough to supply and feed the many thousands of men and women who worked in this industry.

In more recent times, with the political ceasefire and Belfast businesses welcoming tourists to their doors, we noticed some hotels and small restaurants popping up that wanted to sell fresh seafood. This was the start of what has been described as the Ewing institution. We focused on quality and service for the personal touch and are now supplying all northern Ireland's top hotels and restaurants with fresh seafood daily. We have a growing customer base of over 400 clients and almost 300 of these receive deliveries every day via a fleet of refrigerated vans.

Ewing Seafoods understand the importance of sourcing local, and the provenance of our products is very important. It's no secret that the fishing ports in Ireland aren't what they were 100 years ago; it's a difficult and unpredictable industry that has faced many challenges over the years. However, we have been doing this for a long time now and have many good relationships with fishermen and the ports they operate from, meaning we get the finest choice of fish every day. We pride ourselves on good friendships and quick payment! We source fresh seafood from all of Ireland's ports including Kilkeel, Portavogie and Ardglass.

We are proud to hold and have maintained many accreditations and awards over the years, including BRC, AA, Great Taste and the Top 50 Foods in the UK and Ireland. The recipe we have shared for this book is Lavinia Ewing's favourite, borrowed from the wonderful Paula McIntyre. We hope you enjoy it.

PALE SMOKED HADDOCK SCOTCH EGG

This is a wonderful recipe using our delicious pale smoked haddock to make a scotch egg, as opposed to sausage meat. It's lovely served with a homemade parsley mayonnaise for dipping.

300g pale smoked haddock

35g cream cheese

2 scallions, finely chopped

1 tbsp chopped fresh dill

Salt and pepper

4 small eggs

100g plain flour

1 large egg

2 tbsp milk

150g breadcrumbs

Oil, for frying

Sea salt, to finish

Preheat your oven to 180°c and brush a baking tray with oil. Place the smoked haddock on the tray and cook in the oven for about 10 minutes. Remove and leave to cool.

Once cool, flake the smoked haddock and remove any bones and skin. Place the fish in a food processor with the cream cheese, scallions and dill. Blend until smooth and then season to taste.

While the haddock is cooking, boil the 4 small eggs in their shells for 5 minutes, then plunge them straight into iced water to prevent discolouration.

Once cooled, peel the eggs and pat dry. Take a quarter of the haddock mix and flatten it in the palm of your hand, which ideally should be cold, and place an egg in the middle. Mould the haddock mix into a ball to completely cover the egg, then repeat with the remainder.

Leave the eggs like this to rest for up to an hour. Meanwhile, place the flour in one bowl, whisk the remaining large egg with the milk in another, and place the breadcrumbs in a third bowl.

Coat the rested scotch eggs in the flour, then the egg mix, then the breadcrumbs. Heat a deep fat fryer or a large pan half full of oil to 200°c and cook the eggs for 3 minutes until golden brown. Drain on kitchen paper to remove excess oil, then serve warm and enjoy with some parsley mayonnaise.

FISH CITY

BY AARON NORTON

"Led by husband-and-wife team Grainne and John Lavery, we began our journey in 2013 as a fish and chip restaurant in Ballynahinch and partnered with the Marine Stewardship Council (MSC) to become the first MSC certified restaurant on the island of Ireland."

We at Fish City are passionate about ensuring that future generations can experience the wide variety of fish and seafood available to us now, from popular favourites like cod and haddock to lesser-known species, molluscs, and crustacea. Sustainability and responsible sourcing have been at the heart of our family business from the very beginning.

Led by husband-and-wife team Grainne and John Lavery, we began our journey in 2013 as a fish and chip restaurant in Ballynahinch and partnered with the Marine Stewardship Council (MSC) to become the first MSC certified restaurant on the island of Ireland. We moved to Belfast in 2016 and further expanded on our concept of combining sustainably sourced fish and chip shop classics with a seafood fine dining experience, complemented by a carefully curated wine list and expertly served with the warmest of Northern Irish hospitality. We are honoured at the recognition of Fish City as the UK's Restaurant of the Year and Environment & Sustainability Champion at the National Fish & Chip Awards 2023.

As members of the Marine Conservation Society, we are committed to protecting our oceans and the marine ecosystems our seafood comes from. From our kitchen, we champion locally sourced produce from Northern Irish farms and fisheries to reduce food miles and improve the environmental integrity of our dishes. Our guests can enjoy a wide range of fresh local seafood, from Carlingford oysters and Strangford mussels to Irish sea trout and County Down cockles. Our innovative chefs expertly craft dishes with an array of local and seasonal produce, including Red Bay lobster, Dundrum Bay clams, Ballycastle scallops, and Portavogie prawns.

Education is an important part of our advocacy, which extends from our team to our guests and communities. We maintain an up-to-date Seafood Matrix detailing the provenance of all the seafood we source, ensuring that our Front of House staff are knowledgeable when serving our guests. As the first business to join Sustainable Fish Cities NI, an environmental campaign led by Ulster Wildlife and Nourish NI, we encourage other businesses and organisations to prioritise seafood sustainability across their supply chains. We are also very proud to run an educational Kids Club for local P7 schoolchildren to learn about seafood sustainability and how collectively we can make choices that minimise our impact on the oceans and the environment.

BOUILLABAISSE

· ·

An iconic Provençal fish soup originally made by Marseillaise fishermen, bouillabaisse derives its abundant flavour from boiling and reducing rockfish in a fragrant broth. At Fish City, we substitute the salmon in this recipe with sustainably sourced sea trout.

1 onion, finely sliced

1 white leek, finely sliced

1 stick of celery, finely chopped

1 fennel bulb, finely sliced

45ml olive oil

250ml white wine

2 bay leaves

1 sprig of thyme

1 star anise

1 orange, zested

Pinch of saffron

1.5 litres fish stock

500g tinned chopped tomatoes

35ml Pernod

1 mackerel fillet, cut into 4 pieces

4 x 80g salmon fillets

4 large langoustines

12 mussels

1 fresh baguette

5 cloves of garlic

Sweat off all the vegetables in the olive oil until soft.

Add the wine, herbs, star anise, orange zest, and saffron to the pan. Reduce the liquid by 75%.

Add the fish stock and chopped tomatoes to the pan, then cook over a gentle heat for 2 hours.

Remove the pan from the heat and add the Pernod, then season with salt and pepper to taste.

Pan fry the mackerel and salmon, then add the langoustines so that everything finishes cooking at the same time. Meanwhile, cook the mussels in the bouillabaisse until they open.

To make the garlic croutes, cut the baguette into 1cm slices, rub with olive oil and a garlic clove, then bake in the oven at 180°c for 4-5 minutes.

Serve the bouillabaisse with your garlic croutes and some red pepper aioli.

PREPARATION TIME: APPROXIMATELY 30 MINUTES | COOKING TIME: 2 HOURS | SERVES 4

THE FISH WORKS

BY TIFFANY IRVIN

"Mainland Scotland has over six thousand miles of coastline and over two thousand registered fishing vessels, yet Scotland exports 80% of the seafood caught in its waters. This is why we believe in using locally sourced produce as much as possible."

The Fish Works was established in 2017 by myself and my husband Ross. We had toyed with the idea of opening our own fish and chip shop for many years but having no experience whatsoever in the fish and chip industry and not nearly enough savings, we held off. After my dad asked why we hadn't taken the leap and I explained our fear and lack of funds, he kindly offered us a loan to get The Fish Works started. Being foodies, we knew exactly the type of food we wanted to produce and how our branding would look. We wanted to create somewhere locals and visitors could come to enjoy fresh quality Scottish seafood in a relaxed environment, with the best views of the Firth of Clyde.

Ross and I now run The Fish Works with the most fantastic team; we could not do it without them and love passing on our knowledge and passion. We have an excellent fryer in Ozkan Kavak who holds the fort when we cannot be there. Being a family business and having two young children, our team help us more than they will ever know.

Our produce is delivered daily and we only cook to order, allowing us to produce only the best quality food that's always cooked to perfection, from our traditional fish and chips to our locally caught langoustine. Mainland Scotland has over six thousand miles of coastline and over two thousand registered fishing vessels, yet Scotland exports 80% of the seafood caught in its waters. This is why we believe in using locally sourced produce as much as possible, which includes our potatoes, black pudding and haggis.

The Fish Works also has an environmental policy we are extremely proud of; from oil recycling to beach cleans and biodegradable packaging, the business is always striving to lower its carbon footprint. We are dedicated to our community too, which has earned two Early Day Motions in Westminster. This sits alongside our many awards, including third place in the National Fish and Chip Awards 2023, Best Family Operated Fish and Chip Shop in Scotland, a Taste our Best Award for five years running from Visit Scotland, our Green Tourism Award, and the National Federation of Fish Fryers Quality Award Champion Winner at The National Fish and Chip Awards 2023, to name just a few! We believe that our success is down to our pride in providing the best experience with amazing food.

Today's Potatoes: Agria
4 Corners farm Pymoor, Ely, England.

Today's Boat: Shalimar
Sustainably Sourced, Landed & Hand filleted in Peterhead

BLACK PUI
HAGGIS FI
SAUSAGES
CHICKEN E
HOMEMADE
FISH WORK
CURRY SA

THE FISH WORKS

COMFORTING SMOKED HADDOCK
MACARONI & CHEESE

· ·

This is a family favourite of ours that first made its way into The Fish Works on the specials board during Seafood Week 2017. It quickly became a customer favourite, enjoyed by all ages: everyone loves mac and cheese but adding smoked haddock makes it even better.

75g panko breadcrumbs

1 tbsp dried parsley

300g short pasta

4 tbsp butter

1 clove of garlic, finely chopped

1 tsp mustard powder

3 tbsp plain flour

600ml milk

300g mature cheddar, grated (don't use pre-grated cheese as it contains additional starch)

4 undyed smoked haddock fillets, cut into 3-4cm chunks

Salt and ground black pepper

Fresh parsley sprigs, for decoration

1 large French baguette, cut into slices

Salted butter, for the bread

Preheat the oven to 200°c or 180°c fan. In a bowl, mix the panko breadcrumbs with the dried parsley and set aside.

Cook the pasta for 2 minutes less than stated by the guidelines on the packet, as it will be finished off in the oven, then drain and set aside.

Meanwhile, melt the butter in a separate large pan. Stir in the garlic and mustard powder, then lightly simmer to release the flavours for about 1 minute.

Add the flour to the flavoured butter and mix thoroughly to create a roux. Cook for a further minute, then begin adding the milk a little at a time, whisking constantly to create a lump-free sauce. Once all the milk has been incorporated, simmer the sauce for 4 minutes while whisking to allow it to thicken.

Remove the pan from the heat, add the grated cheddar and stir until the cheese is all melted. Once the cheese has fully melted, put the pan back on a low heat and begin adding the smoked haddock.

Allow the smoked haddock to poach in the cheese sauce for 3 minutes, then stir in the cooked pasta. Season the mixture to taste with salt and black pepper but be aware that you will not need a lot of salt, if any, as the smoked haddock adds tons of flavour.

Transfer the mixture to an ovenproof dish or 4 smaller ovenproof dishes if you wish to make individual portions, then sprinkle the parsley breadcrumbs on top. Bake the macaroni cheese in the preheated oven for 15 minutes until the breadcrumbs begin to turn golden.

To serve, spoon onto 4 plates or place individual dishes on heatproof plates and garnish with the fresh parsley. My family love having this on a cold winter's night, served up with freshly cut slices of French baguette topped with lashings of salted butter.

PREPARATION TIME: 10 MINUTES | COOKING TIME: 40 MINUTES | SERVES 4

FISHING INTO THE FUTURE

BY ADRIAN BARTLETT, FITF VICE CHAIR

"For too long fishermen's knowledge, experience and ideas have been side-lined, and it's our mission to ensure that everyone has the right knowledge, skills and connections to integrate into fisheries management and cast their voice."

Fishing into the Future is a UK charity created by fishermen, for fishermen. We are led by forward-thinking people who work in the fishing industry to create learning experiences where people in the industry, scientists and decision makers can share knowledge and create connections that enable shared participation, effective dialogue, and mutual understanding. Our recipe for success is in-person events and workshops, supported by regular fishermen-led conversations online and a one-stop-shop website to inform and connect (www.fishingporthole.co.uk) but the secret ingredient is the authentic human connections we create when fishermen, scientists and fisheries managers break bread together.

We have a shared goal of prosperous and sustainable fisheries, but the diverse selection of people working in UK fisheries don't always see eye to eye in attempts to achieve this. We believe our best chance of success is through co-management. This means that everyone is onboard to participate in fisheries management, and the science used in decision making. For too long fishermen's knowledge, experience and ideas have been side-lined, and it's our mission to ensure that everyone has the right knowledge, skills and connections to integrate into fisheries management and cast their voice.

Adrian, a retired fisherman, also promotes industry safety, works with an initiative to reduce carbon emissions in the fishing fleet, and hosts regular cooking demonstrations at seafood shows around the country. He joined the charity as a trustee after attending a FITF workshop and is vice-chair to our industry-led Board of Trustees. At FITF, we truly believe we are at an exciting time here, where co-management is a hot topic that everyone is getting onboard with. The industry is paving its way in participatory processes, such as Fisheries Management Plans, and it's our job to lay the foundations so everyone – not just fishermen, but also the people working in science and government – is able to work together in the best possible way.

As a charity, we aim to bring fishermen's knowledge to the forefront and ensure that underrepresented groups have a seat at the table, so spotlighting the humble whelk in our recipe for this book fits well with our mission. Not a species you will frequently find in cookbooks, we had to dig deep into the traditional knowledge from our Board of Trustees, the vast majority being active fishermen and people working in the seafood supply chain. These board members give their time voluntarily while also running fishing businesses to be part of our movement towards long-term, sustainable, and prosperous fisheries.

WHELKS WITH CHILLI GARLIC BUTTER

· ·

Whelks are a hugely underrated, sustainable, and low-impact seafood choice. They are caught in the UK and mostly exported to Europe and Asia, where they are sold as an aphrodisiac. We can't promise that's not a clever marketing ploy, but they do have a delicious briny-sweet flavour that pairs well with this bold dipping sauce.

Butter

Fresh garlic, peeled and crushed

Fresh chilli, finely chopped (or chilli flakes)

4-5 whelks (about 50g of meat) per person

Fresh lemons or limes

Crusty bread, to serve

For the chilli garlic butter

Gently heat the butter in a small saucepan until the butter melts and starts to foam. Add the crushed garlic, then remove the pan from the heat immediately. Stir in a small pinch of salt and a generous pinch of chopped chilli, or chilli flakes. Taste to check the seasoning and then set aside so the flavours meld together while you cook the whelks.

For the whelks

If you live near or are visiting the coast, we recommend you ask around for whelks from local dayboats between January and September. Otherwise, ask your local independent fishmonger or search online for suppliers that can send whelks through the post.

If cooking the whelks from fresh with the shells on, they should be rinsed several times in their shells, changing the water between rinses, to remove dirt and grit. You also want to remove their inner track before eating, by simply slicing the whelk, pulling the hard waste track from the back of the whelk (and discarding), then washing the whelk. One trick of the trade is to freeze fresh whelks, at least overnight, before cooking them. This breaks down the proteins, making them more tender.

Whelks can be steamed at high temperature or boiled from fresh or frozen and we recommend asking your fishmonger for guidance on cooking times. Put the clean whelks into a large pan of heavily salted cold water and bring to a simmer, if you have bought cooked whelk meat you just have to defrost the meat and warm it up. If cooking from fresh, it's recommended that they are not simmered for longer than 10 minutes. Be careful not to overcook the whelks to avoid them becoming rubbery and tough.

Once cooked, squeeze a generous amount of fresh lemon or lime juice over the whelk meat before serving with extra lemon or lime wedges, crusty bread and a beer. Don't forget seafood forks or pickers to get the meat out the shells, otherwise supply plenty of napkins!

THE GIRLYFISHMONGER

BY EMMA MCKEATING

"There aren't many female fishmongers in this industry. I think when people think of the role of a fishmonger, they assume it's a man's job. I am very proud to be an Advanced Fishmonger on The Master Fishmonger Standard."

I have been a fishmonger since December 2013. Prior to that, I hated fish! As a young girl, I refused to eat fish and would try to hide it amongst vegetables on the plate… My parents saw the importance of having fish in your diet, but I definitely didn't! Things changed when I worked in a supermarket and – to cut a long story short – trained as a fishmonger. Ever since, I have been constantly learning more about the fishing industry and how to try and encourage people of all ages to eat more fish. If I can find a love of fish, anyone can!

My parents play a massive role in my career, as they are both so supportive of what I do, especially when I travel all over the country to learn more and teach others while doing demonstrations at festivals. I also have to credit Alexander, who started my training, as one of the most patient teachers I have ever known. Every single fisherman I have ever met continues to be a source of inspiration, none more so than one of my greatest inspirations, Sarah Ready, who has worked with inshore fishing fleets for over 30 years.

I am very passionate about the fishing industry and I don't think, as a whole, we understand and appreciate the hard work and sacrifice undertaken to get fish on our plates. There aren't many female fishmongers in this industry. I think when people think of the role of a fishmonger, they assume it's a man's job. I am very proud to be an Advanced Fishmonger on The Master Fishmonger Standard. As I'm so passionate about the fishing industry, I try my best to use local produce, such as locally caught crab which I hand dress and have found is very popular due to the amazing flavour.

SMOKED HADDOCK KEDGEREE

· ·

This is the first recipe I ever cooked! The mango chutney is a game changer as it adds a little sweetness. The finished kedgeree can also be eaten cold, making it perfect for any time of the day.

500g smoked haddock

568ml (1 pint) fish stock

1 bay leaf

1 tsp butter

1 onion, chopped

2 cardamom pods, crushed

1 tsp ground turmeric

1 tsp curry powder

350g cooked basmati rice

4 boiled eggs, quartered

Mango chutney, to serve

Place the haddock skin side up in a shallow pan over a low heat. Cover with the fish stock and add the bay leaf. Gently poach the fish for approximately 5-7 minutes, then turn off the heat and let it stand for 10 minutes.

Transfer the fish to a plate, saving the poaching liquid, and remove the skin. The fish should flake easily using your fingers or a fork. Pour the liquid into a jug and set aside for later.

Melt the butter in the pan, then add the chopped onion and fry until softened. Add the cardamom, turmeric and curry powder to cook gently for 3 minutes.

Add the cooked rice, flaked haddock and reserved fish stock to the pan. Gently heat through until the liquid starts to reduce. Don't stir too much as the fish will start to break up.

Finally, add the boiled eggs to the kedgeree and serve warm with some mango chutney.

THE HAND PICKED SCALLOP COMPANY LTD

....

BY FRAZER PUGH

"We are a team of five ocean-loving amphibians who spend our time underwater harvesting what Mother Nature provides in a respectful way, as well as educating as many people as possible about how important it is to learn where our food comes from and the detrimental effect it often has on our planet."

My life as a scallop diver began in 2015. I was living in Germany after returning from three years in Australasia, where I travelled while teaching diving. After learning to live in my true environment, below the shoreline – despite my disadvantage of not having been born with gills – I had found my home.

After researching the damage that dredging for scallops does to the underwater environment, which is likened to burning down a rainforest to catch a parrot, I realised that I could make a difference by providing eco-minded foodies with a non-destructive way of sourcing an extremely popular seafood.

So, I returned to England to pursue a job as a scallop diver. From there I managed to find four days' work experience on a dive boat in Devon and decided I would build a boat and run my own operation. There aren't many of us around, mainly due to the "self-preservation" properties that most people possess, so it is very difficult to find employment as a scallop diver.

Seven seasons later, we are a team of five ocean-loving amphibians who spend our time underwater harvesting what Mother Nature provides in a respectful way, as well as educating as many people as possible about how important it is to learn where our food comes from and the detrimental effect it often has on our planet.

The ethos of The Hand Picked Scallop Company is to harvest the best shellfish that nature has to offer while causing no damage to the underwater environment. We achieve this through diving and selecting each shell that we pick up by hand. This is driven by a passion to change the way people are connected to their food and the story of how it got to their plate. Our future aim is to build a fleet of boats all governed by the same core ethics.

SEARED SCALLOPS IN HERBY GARLIC BUTTER

···

This recipe for our hand dived scallops is very simple, as we believe they should be enjoyed as naturally as possible, to savour their sweet and delicious flavour.

3 scallops per serving

Salt and pepper

Butter

Garlic, minced

Fresh herbs of your choice

Season the scallops on both sides with salt and pepper, then sear in a hot pan with foaming butter for 2 minutes on each side.

Mince the garlic, finely chop the herbs, then add both to the pan when the scallops are almost cooked. Toss gently to combine all the flavours, then serve immediately.

We recommend enjoying these seared buttery scallops with wedges of lemon on the side for squeezing over the juice, to add a little freshness to the dish.

INKA CRESSWELL

WILDLIFE FILMMAKER AND MARINE BIOLOGIST

"By combining arts with science, I hoped to use storytelling to shed light on the incredible biologists, fisherfolk and activists working on the front lines of ocean conservation."

For as long as I can remember, I have been captivated by our oceans. I grew up in Brighton and some of my earliest memories are swimming in the sea, barbecuing with family on the beach as we watched the sunset, and searching rock pools until the tide came in. Rock pooling and beach combing in search of mermaid's purses and other ocean treasures was my first glimpse into the magic, wonder and adventure our oceans hold.

By age six, I was already determined to become a marine biologist. It was that passion, sparked at a young age and nurtured by my parents, that lead me to university to pursue my dream. Throughout my studies, however, I became more aware of the disconnect between science and general awareness and wanted to do more to educate people about the need for conservation action. By combining arts with science, I hoped to use storytelling to shed light on the incredible biologists, fisherfolk and activists working on the front lines of ocean conservation.

I now work as a wildlife filmmaker and underwater photographer. My work has led me to explore a huge variety of ocean ecosystems from kelp forests and seagrass beds to polar ice fields, thriving coral reefs, open ocean, and even deep hydrothermal vent fields. Each ecosystem has its own unique character and I always feel so privileged to be able to spend time unlocking the secrets of all these habitats. I often get to collaborate with incredible scientists and spend extended periods of time watching and learning from these habitats and local experts.

My favourite part of my work is deciphering marine life behaviour. By breaking down these complex interactions, I'm able to see these ecosystems in an entirely new light and gain a new appreciation for the importance of every part. My first independent film – My 25: The Ocean Between Us, which was selected for several international film festivals – explored the importance of marine protected areas built in collaboration with local fishing communities and how coastal communities can recover after being impacted by unsustainable fishing practices. I wanted to highlight the importance of indigenous knowledge as well as cutting-edge science and the potential to restore our wild blue spaces.

As an avid ocean conservationist, I'm always looking for ways to eat more sustainably and for me, this means eating locally and supporting sustainable fishing practices. I hope you are inspired to do the same by the recipes in this book, including my mum's jerked mackerel on the next page.

JO'S JERKED MACKEREL

As a kid, we used to catch mackerel with my dad locally and my mum Jo would put together the most incredible jerk seasoning and barbecue them on the beach over the bonfire. As a mixed Jamaican/British family it was the perfect fusion of culture and home.

2 limes, 1 juiced and 1 quartered

4 mackerel, cleaned (heads on or off)

2 large onions

2-3 cloves of garlic

For the jerk seasoning

1 scotch bonnet pepper, seeds removed (use half if you don't want it too hot)

1 onion, quartered

2 tbsp soy sauce

1 tbsp vegetable or olive oil

1 tbsp dried thyme

2 tsp allspice berries or powder

2 tsp ground cumin

1 tsp paprika

1 tsp brown sugar

For the jerk seasoning, blend all the ingredients together in a blender or pestle and mortar. Combine this with the lime juice in a bowl.

Use a sharp knife to make two diagonal cuts on one side of each mackerel, then place the fish in the bowl of jerk seasoning and rub all over until completely coated.

Halve and slice the remaining onions, then mix them with the fish and jerk seasoning. Peel and crush the garlic cloves, add them to the bowl, then leave to marinate for a few hours.

Lay the marinated mackerel on a baking tray in a row or head to tail, cut side up. Scatter the sliced onions all around the fish, then cover the tray with foil or greaseproof paper.

Bake in a hot oven or on a barbecue for 15 minutes, or until the eyes are white (if the heads have been left on) and remove the foil for the last few minutes.

Serve the baked or barbecued mackerel with the lime wedges. It goes well with plain boiled rice and a lovely mixed leaf salad, or even just a baguette at a barbecue.

Tip: For the most sustainable mackerel, choose hook and line (handline) caught and always release juvenile mackerel if fishing for them yourself.

ISLA GALE

SCALLOP TRAWLER APPRENTICE SKIPPER, ISLE OF MAN

"Initially a lot of my friends thought my passion for going to sea was a little strange and couldn't understand why I wanted to join a male-dominated industry – away from home for weeks with long hours, hard work and dangerous conditions – but I just loved it."

Born and raised on the Isle of Man, I grew up going out on my dad's fishing boat, dropping rods off the side catching mackerel and callig (the Manx word for pollock). That was where my passion for being at sea was born and from primary school age, I wanted to be the first female skipper of a scallop/queenie trawler on the Isle of Man. When I reached 12, I started going out with my dad on his trawler, June Rose, on weekends and school holidays and would take every opportunity to learn from him. At 15, I was offered an apprentice position by another skipper in the fleet and after some long discussions with my mum (who was still hoping it was a phase) as well as taking my GCSE study leave on the boat, I was packed and ready to go full time as soon as my last exam was completed.

Initially a lot of my friends thought my passion for going to sea was a little strange and couldn't understand why I wanted to join a male-dominated industry – away from home for weeks with long hours, hard work and dangerous conditions – but I just loved it. I would get lots of strange looks when we landed into ports but when they saw me working the winches and landing, I think they saw I was more than able. Winning the Fishing News Trainee Fisherman of the Year Award in May 2022 helped to validate that I wasn't just along for the ride but capable, dedicated and passionate about the job.

Now in my second year aboard the Shannon Kimberly with my skipper Alan, we fish on the West Coast of Scotland and around the Isle of Man dredging for scallops. The grounds are managed to avoid overfishing and areas are closed to encourage regrowth and support breeding stocks. There's increased awareness which is improving practices and management of the grounds. As well as working towards my Class 2 skipper's ticket, the future of the industry is incredibly important to me. I want to be an ambassador for not only girls looking to enter the industry but all young people, improving pathways for them to get involved and demonstrating that there are viable career options open if you're prepared to put in the work. I recognise as a skipper that bringing your crew home safe is as important as bringing a catch home. I don't just want to be the first female skipper; I want to be a good skipper!

MANX SCALLOPS WITH CHARRED LITTLE GEM LETTUCE AND CREAMY SAUCE

This lovely starter is all made in one frying pan. If you want to make it a main course, simply increase the number of scallops and add potatoes and a vegetable of your choice.

6 Manx scallops

20g butter

20ml olive oil

1 banana shallot, finely chopped

6 cloves of garlic, 2 finely chopped and 4 finely sliced

1 Little Gem lettuce, quartered

100ml good white wine

100ml double cream

Wash and dry the scallops. Preheat the oven to 100°c (80°c fan) and put an ovenproof dish in to warm along with the plates you will be serving the dish on.

Heat half the butter and oil in a medium size frying pan and gently fry the shallot and chopped garlic until cooked through. Remove from the pan and put to one side.

In the same pan, heat the remaining butter and oil. Increase the heat and when bubbling, add the sliced garlic and stir round for a minute or so until it starts to colour. Add the quarters of lettuce and char quickly on the two cut sides. Quickly transfer the lettuce and garlic to the warm dish in the oven.

In the same pan, cook the scallops to a good colour on both sides. This should take about a minute on each side. Transfer them to the dish in the oven alongside the lettuce.

Pour the wine into the frying pan and reduce by half, then add the cream and allow it to bubble and reduce.

To serve, place the scallops and lettuce on the warm plates. Scatter the garlic slices over the lettuce. Drizzle some of the sauce over the scallops, serving the remainder in a jug on the side.

PREPARATION TIME: 15 MINUTES | COOKING TIME: 15 MINUTES | SERVES 2 AS A STARTER

ISLAND FISH

BY AMANDA PENDER

"Island Fish is committed to the future of fishing in Scilly; our ancestors made it possible for us to follow in their footsteps and we believe it is our duty to ensure the same for the next generation."

The Pender family has been fishing out of Bryher for hundreds of years and Island Fish has been continuing this proud family tradition since it was established by myself and my brother Mark in 2015. Three generations of Penders are now following in the footsteps of our ancestors, supplying quality lobster, crab, wet fish and shellfish across the Isles of Scilly that we would argue are some of the freshest and most affordable you can find anywhere in the country.

Mark and our father Mike go out daily to fish the waters around Scilly in their boats, The Emerald Dawn (which Mike built himself) and the Dorothy Ethel, supported by 22 year old Shamus Pender-Frazer and his father Andy Frazer in their boat, the Ma Vie. They drop their 'pots' anywhere from Bishop Rock to the Eastern Isles to bring in local fish and shellfish from April through to December. The catch is either stored at sea in wooden 'carbs' until needed or brought ashore daily for our shop. Myself and my mum Sue cook and pick the crab twice a day, starting around 5am to produce a range of shellfish treats before we open the shop at 9:30.

Island Fish is committed to the future of fishing in Scilly; our ancestors made it possible for us to follow in their footsteps and we believe it is our duty to ensure the same for the next generation. All our mackerel and pollock is caught on hand lines, meaning that there is zero by-catch. At the end of the day, any remaining fish is used either as bait for our lobster pots, for our supper, or to feed Simba the family cat! Our primary method of fishing is potting, again a methodology that has little impact on the seabed, resulting in little if any by-catch.

We in turn are committed to buying locally where we can, working with others to strengthen our island community, not just for us but for the next generation of islanders and visitors to enjoy. Our goal is to ensure that Bryher remains a healthy working and welcoming community with opportunities for life, work, family, and truly spectacular holidays! For us, the magic ingredients are a superlative product, hard work, and passion for a way of life we all believe in and want to share with our customers.

© James Churchill

Photo © James Churchill

SUE'S BRYHER CRAB QUICHE

....

One of the easiest and tastiest of ways to cook crab, guaranteed to tempt even the most shellfish averse members of the family. This simple crab quiche is perfect for al fresco picnics. Serve with a fresh green salad and a cold white wine – you can imagine you are here on the islands enjoying the very best that life has to offer.

1 ½ oz lard

1 ½ oz margarine

6 oz plain flour

Pinch of salt

4 spring onions

100g white crab meat

3 eggs

¼ pint evaporated milk

¼ pint fresh milk

Grated nutmeg, to taste

Handful of grated cheese

Salt and pepper

Grease a 6-inch quiche dish with a little margarine.

In a large bowl, rub the lard, margarine, flour and salt together until well mixed. Add just enough water to make a dough.

Place the dough on a floured board and roll it out to line your quiche dish.

Slice the spring onions and scatter them over the pastry base, then add the crab meat. Whisk the eggs with both types of milk, adding nutmeg for seasoning.

Pour your egg mixture into the quiche case, then sprinkle the top with cheese. Season with salt and pepper to taste.

Bake the quiche in a preheated oven at 180°c for approximately 30-40 minutes. This is perfect served hot or cold.

PREPARATION TIME: 20 MINUTES | COOKING TIME: 40 MINUTES | SERVES 2-3

JADE-S FISHERIES JERSEY

BY GABBY MASON, CO-FOUNDER

"We love everything about Jersey seafood and the Jersey fishing community, from the people to the variety of catch and its exceptional sustainability."

As islanders, we're both intrinsically connected to the sea. It has a magnetic pull we can't deny, so for us, a life dedicated to life on the sea seems natural. Leyton has been a fisherman since his teens and when we met, some years ago now, he brought me into this incredible world and community which I instantly fell in love with. We began Jade-S Fisheries in March 2020; it was our way to survive the export closures caused by Covid-19 and Brexit, and our way to help support our fellow Jersey fishermen and friends.

We named the company after our boat, the Jade-S, to highlight the traceability of our products. We sell what we catch directly to the local market, and we also sell the catches of other local fishermen. We pride ourselves on our knowledge, our quality, and our freshness, all of which can't be beaten. It all comes directly from our local waters and local boats, and goes straight to the customer. We have been able to bring local seafood to the Jersey market – something which, before we began, was a scarcity – and today we have built the reputation as having the best quality local seafood.

We live, eat, sleep, breathe and even dream fishing. We do it all from fishing the boats together, processing and filleting to cooking and smoking, then selling (and all the rest)! We love to do things a little differently, so we sell the catches from our Vintage Citroen HY Van which we drive around the island each weekend. We also supply a selection of local hotels and restaurants, including our own beach café called Driftwood at Archirondel. People are usually surprised that it's just the two of us running the show along with our full-time crab-picker Isabelle… who quite possibly has the hardest task!

We love everything about Jersey seafood and the Jersey fishing community, from the people to the variety of catch and its exceptional sustainability. We hope that we can help shape an industry which continues to survive but also strives for a future for the next generation… but if we can have fun while we do it, even better! We're here for a short time not a long one, and we just love that we get to do it together.

Photo © Matt Sharp

Photo © David Ferguson

Photo © Paul Gregory

Photo © BAM Perspectives

Photo © Matt Sharp

Photo © Matt Sharp

Photo © Paul Gregory

Photo © BAM Perspectives

Photo © David Ferguson

PAN-FRIED SILVER MULLET
WITH JERSEY ROYALS

· ·

Our favourite fish is the Silver Mullet (aka Grey Mullet). It's a true underdog, but its meatiness and incredible flavour can't be denied. It can be best described as a cross between mackerel and bass. This simple recipe will be sure to impress and can easily become a weekly staple.

2 Silver Mullet fillets (2 large fillets or 4 small cuts)

Jersey sea salt and black pepper, to taste

500g Jersey Royals (the smallest are the best for flavour)

Olive oil, for frying

2 tsp Jersey salted butter, plus extra for serving

Greens, vegetables, or salad of your choice

1 lemon

Preheat the oven to 170°c fan. Check your fillets fit in your chosen frying pan – if they're too long cut them in half – as you don't want the fish lying up the sides. Make diagonal cuts along the skin – this helps to stop it curling in the pan. Season both sides with Jersey sea salt and black pepper.

Bring a saucepan of water to the boil, add salt, and then add the Jersey Royals. For a traditional Jersey touch, add fresh mint leaves.

Put a relatively generous amount of olive oil in a frying pan over a high heat. Once hot, add the fish fillets skin side down. If you can't fit them all in one, go don't worry as we will be putting the fried fillet in the oven before serving so you have time. Don't move the fillets at first, allowing the skin to cook and crisp up. Once it has, begin to move them and the oil around the pan to stop the fillets from sticking.

When the fish is almost cooked (you will see a texture and colour change) add the Jersey butter; this adds more flavour but also brings a beautifully golden glow to the fillets. After the fillets are cooked (how long depends on the size of each fillet, but it should be about 15 minutes), reduce the oven temperature to around 120°c. Place the fillets on a tray and pop them in the oven for 8-10 minutes.

Boil your greens of choice (we use broccoli and green beans from the local farmer) and check your Royals are cooked. If they are, remove them from the saucepan and add a generous amount of Jersey butter over them. On our island, this is a must!

Season the greens with some Jersey sea salt and remove the fish from the oven. Plate the fish, Jersey Royals and greens. Cut the lemon into quarters, squeeze the juice from one quarter over the fish and add the remaining quarters to the plate. All you need to accompany the dish is the fresh lemon, as the flavour and juiciness of the fish will be more than enough to impress!

The great thing about this recipe is that it can easily be adapted for more or less people. This is a weekly staple in our home, so we hope you enjoy!

PREPARATION TIME: 20 MINUTES | COOKING TIME: 25 MINUTES | SERVES 2 HUNGRY ADULTS

JERSEY SEAFARIS

BY JOSH DEARING

"I like to think I've changed the way people buy their fish in Jersey and it's so good to see more divers and other environmentally conscious younger fisherman coming up the ranks."

When I moved to Jersey at 18, I worked as a local scuba diving instructor and fell in love with all things ocean related. Diving for scallops was my first commercial fishing; I found it exciting and knowing that I could do something I loved while turning it into a business that was ethical, environmentally friendly, and had zero bycatch made it even more special. 2016 saw the arrival of my boat, BOUNTY, and the start of my ethical wholesale fishing company. This boat allowed me to dive and fish, using pots to catch lobster and crab.

My presence on social media got me noticed – I would say I wasn't your typical fisherman! I had most of the high-end restaurants and hundreds of Jersey's locals on my books. People wanted seafood that didn't cause damage to the sea in the way dredging or trawling does and that's what I specialised in. All the scallops were hand-caught by myself and my dad, Mike, and then cut out, packaged up, and delivered. My mum, Julie, would often help with that too. This approach meant that my customers could meet the person who caught their dinner. We even had our own lobster bands (the rubber bands you put on a lobster's claws to stop them from fighting each other or getting hold of your finger!) which matched the bright yellow of my boat, so people would know who caught their lobster.

I'm no longer a fisherman but I look back over those five years of very early starts, rough weather and a few scary moments with fond memories. I like to think I've changed the way people buy their fish in Jersey and it's so good to see more divers and other environmentally conscious younger fisherman coming up the ranks.

My time is still spent on the water though; I now own an amazing company, Jersey Seafaris, alongside two great guys, Dan and Patch. We take people on trips around the Channel Islands and I still get to educate others about my passion for ethical fishing. Jersey Seafaris is the ultimate Jersey adventure, running trips all over the Channel Islands, the outer reefs such as Les Ecréhous and Les Minquiers, and over to France. Three RIBs operate regular trips and charters, and there is a wide range of wildlife to spot, from sea birds to lots of dolphins and seals! There really is a trip for everyone, whether you fancy lunch or dinner in France, day trips down to Les Chausey, visiting an amazing French archipelago, or a quick tour of the North coast to learn about the island's historic past.

Between all of this, I'm also an RNLI volunteer crew member on both the All Weather and inshore lifeboats in St Helier. I did mention that all my time was still spent on the water!

DIVED JERSEY SCALLOPS
WITH PEA AND MINT PURÉE

· ·

A great quick and simple starter my mum would make if we were having a family dinner. Fresh diver-caught scallops can be found in most good fishmongers; don't be afraid to ask about where your fish has come from and the method with which it was caught.

12 hand dived scallops (sometimes referred to as dived or diver-caught scallops)

Small bunch of fresh chives

200ml crème fraîche

500g peas

4 rashers of smoked streaky bacon

A few sprigs of mint

4 scallop shells, to serve

Salt and pepper, to taste

Clean the scallops by cutting off the harder small bit of flesh on the opposite side of the roe, rinsing under water and then dabbing with kitchen roll to dry. If the scallops have the roe on, this will add a nice bright orange colour to the finished dish. Set them aside until ready to cook.

Chop the chives finely and mix them through the crème fraîche. This will go on top of the dish to add a zingy flavour to the scallops.

Place a saucepan of water on the hob and bring to the boil. Pour in all the peas and leave them to cook for about 5 minutes. While the peas boil away, grab a frying pan and start cooking the bacon. The bacon needs to be well cooked to make it crispy and could always be swapped out for pancetta.

Take the peas out of the pan and set half aside to be kept whole. Add the other half to a food processor or a small bowl along with the mint leaves, then pulse or use a hand blender to create a mushy pea consistency. Season the purée to taste with salt and pepper if needed.

Using a second frying pan, it's time to cook the scallops. Heat up some oil over a rather high heat. Once the pan is up to temperature, add the scallops. Some people like to place them in a spiral, so they know which order to turn them over in. The pan should sizzle when you place them in. After 90 seconds the scallops will be ready to turn and should have a crispy skin on the cooked side.

To serve

Place some of the pea purée in the scallop shell or on a small plate if you couldn't get any shells, then add the whole peas. Place 3 scallops on each portion on top of your peas. Take the bacon out of the pan and either crumble or place a rasher over each serving. The chive crème fraiche can then be placed on the top or on the side to finish.

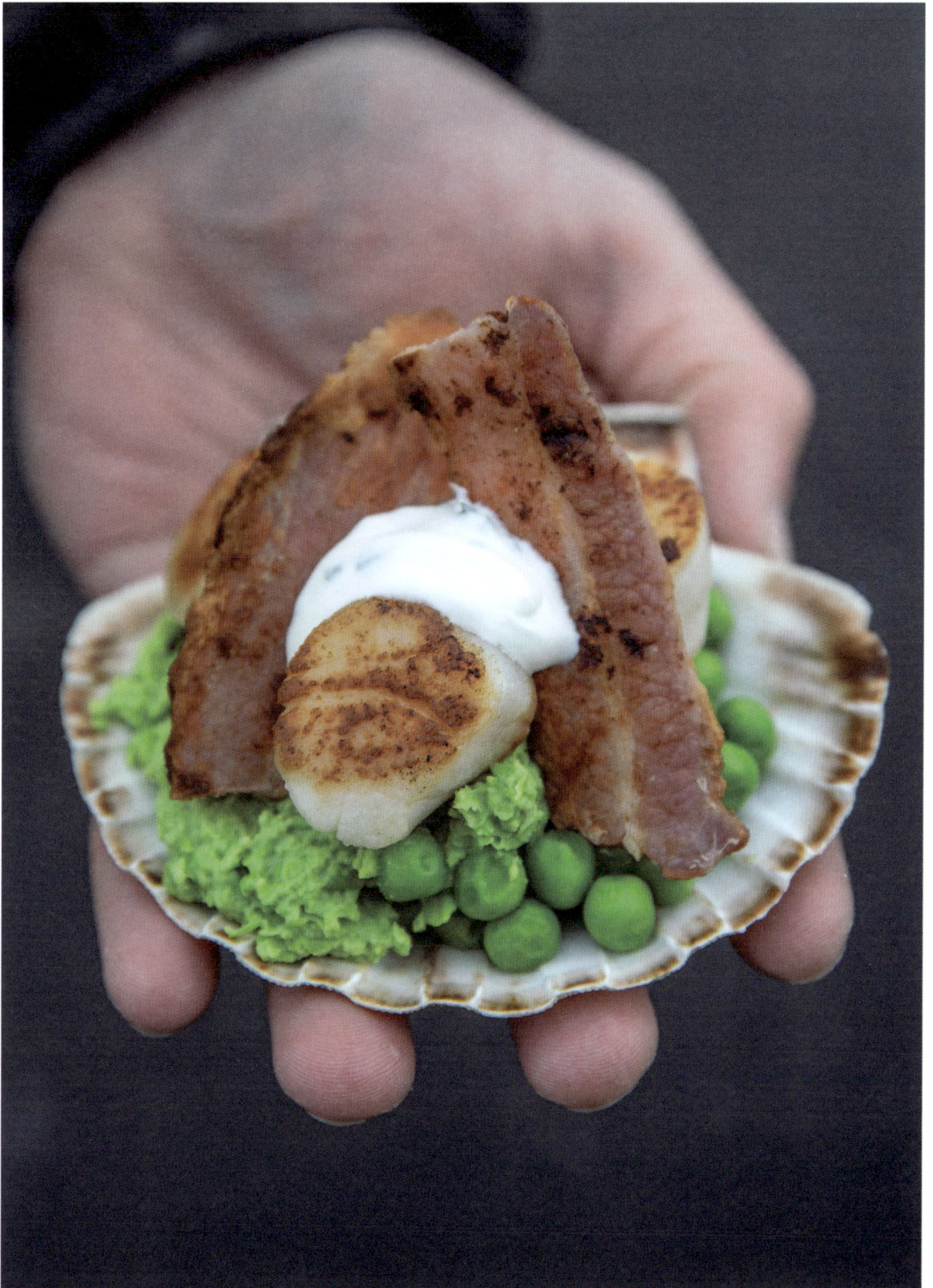

JOHNSONS ENTERPRISES

BY ANDREW JOHNSON

"There are not many fishmongers left so I'd love to see Johnsons Fish still thriving in years to come, with emphasis on quality, freshness, and sustainability at the heart of what we do."

I've been a Saturday boy, a deckhand, a skipper on a trawler, and now I'm the owner of a family-run fish business. Over the years things have changed, but we must move with the times.

My late father, Bernie Johnson, started to evolve the company in the early 70s. Still in school, I remember hardly seeing him. Working all the hours under the sun to get the company going, he was determined to make the business work. Our family originally came from the Isle of Sheppey in Kent, so boats, fishing and the sea have always been a key part of our lives. Originally a shipwright, my father's love for fishing took over his future, with myself following along in his footsteps.

The business has always been family-run, supported by brilliant, loyal, long-serving staff. Our love and passion for fish and the industry has always been paramount in the quality and service we have provided to both our trade and retail customers over the years.

Since 1975, when the company was first registered, we've seen huge changes to the industry. Many highs and many lows, but we've always been 100% committed to supporting our British and local fishing fleets. We fully recognise the efforts and dedication of these men and women as we can say we've been there and done it ourselves, operating a large trawler fleet, catching and landing fish from all around the UK from 1975 to 2000. I skippered some of our trawlers throughout that period myself.

In 2000, when I took over Johnsons Enterprises, the company started supplying trade customers with high quality fresh fish and shellfish, delivering to Hampshire, West Sussex and parts of Surrey.

Around 2012, things changed a little more, as we moved more into the retail area, visiting farm shops with our mobile fish stalls. We now visit 12 stalls per week, promoting our locally caught seafood such as wild bass, plaice, skate wing, Dover sole and much more. The wild hook and line caught seabass has always been a top seller. Now, with our amazing continued support from so many customers, this continues to grow, especially during these challenging times.

I hope to see the company continue to grow and adapt with time. There are not many fishmongers left so I'd love to see Johnsons Fish still thriving in years to come, with emphasis on quality, freshness, and sustainability at the heart of what we do.

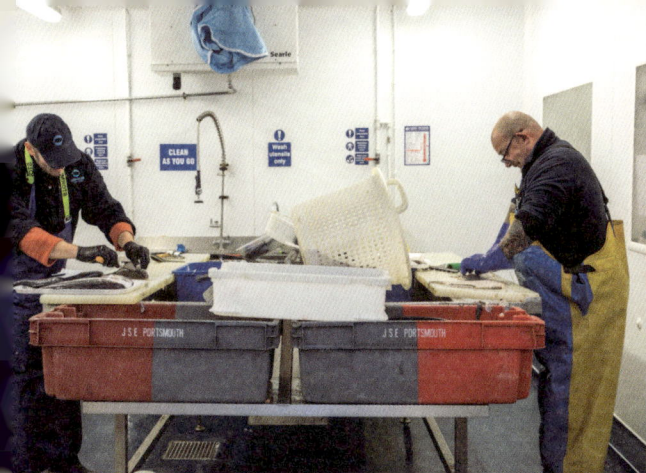

MEDITERRANEAN STYLE
ROASTED WHOLE WILD SEABASS

· ·

This is the perfect one-dish bake. When buying the seabass, ask your fishmonger to gut, scale and remove the gills on your fish but leave the fins on, as this enables you to remove the flesh from the frame more easily.

1 x 800g-1kg wild seabass

8 new potatoes

1 unwaxed lemon, halved

Olive oil, for drizzling

Coarsely ground sea salt, to taste

Coarsely ground black pepper, to taste

Oregano, to taste

1 red pepper, cut into chunky slices

1 yellow pepper, cut into chunky slices

2 vines of ripe cherry tomatoes

100g samphire

Preheat the oven to 200°c and line a baking dish, big enough to stand the whole fish up in, with greaseproof paper.

Score a line through the skin from the head to the tail – down the top of the fish, between the dorsal fins. Then make 3-4 scores through the skin on either side of the seabass.

Bring a saucepan of water to boil, add the new potatoes and parboil them for 2-5 minutes.

Squeeze half the lemon over the fish, then drizzle it with olive oil and season with a good pinch of sea salt, black pepper and oregano. Place your fish upright in the middle of the dish, arranging the parboiled new potatoes and sliced peppers around the fish. Make sure your veggies are well seasoned too. Place your dish into the preheated oven for 10 minutes on the middle shelf.

After 5 minutes, add the cherry vine tomatoes to the pan and squeeze the second half of the lemon over the fish. Increase the oven temperature to 220°c and finish cooking for the last 5 minutes. Just before you get everything out of the oven for the last time, steam the samphire for 30 seconds.

Serve this at the table straight from the pan.

PREPARATION TIME: 5 MINUTES | COOKING TIME: 15 MINUTES | SERVES 2

LAURA N162

· ·

BY LAURA WILKINS

"My own love of the sea started when my dad decided to build a fishing boat in the driveway! 'Laura' was launched the same day I started primary school and I have been fishing onboard it ever since."

My family's love of the sea started with my great-great-grandad being part of the lifeboat crew that responded to the 'Mexico Disaster' in 1886 by rowing out on a dark stormy night to bring stricken seamen home. Unfortunately, on that fateful night, only a few men returned. While even today the sea remains a very dangerous workplace for seafarers, it also connects communities through a unique and special bond; following the Mexico Disaster, the local community held the first RNLI Flag Day.

My own love of the sea started when my dad decided to build a fishing boat in the driveway! 'Laura' was launched the same day I started primary school and I have been fishing onboard it ever since. It will also be no surprise that I followed in the steps of my great-great-grandmother and married a member of the local lifeboat crew! The family boat operates along the Mourne coast, specialising in seasonal shellfish, and is part of a Northern Ireland lobster v-notching scheme, which ensures the long-term sustainability of that fishery. When sourcing bait for our pots, we use mackerel and Mourne Herring. Our shellfish is sold to a local family-operated shellfish processor, from where it can be shipped all over the world.

For me, the Mourne Herring Fishery symbolises a lot of what fishing today represents as well as the unique cultural history our industry has played in shaping towns and communities throughout the UK. Historically in Mourne, once the catch was landed, the herring was salted, placed in large barrels and shipped worldwide. Traditionally, the whole local community was involved in the process in some capacity and therefore benefited both economically and socially. Indeed, people from Mourne became known as 'herring gutters'.

The 'herring gutter' story is also a good example of how the fishing industry and communities, have, like the sea, changed with the seasons and weathered many storms and challenges. Today, this local herring fishery is referred to as a sustainable 'artisan' fishery. However, the sense of fishing community remains strong, with fishermen still coming together to prepare boats and nets, and catching the allocated annual quota by working together. The processed herring continue to be shipped globally, demonstrating that, while fishing may change, the shared connection in our love of the sea, community spirit and support of seafaring charities remains as strong as ever, alongside the aim of a sustainable and productive future fishing industry.

OAT FRIED HERRING

The Mourne Herring I use for this recipe represents a regional, seasonal, sustainable, artisan fishery. Furthermore, the 'herring gutter' story (see the previous page) represents the economic and social fishing heritage and traditions of the fishing communities within the Kingdom of Mourne.

125g butter

2 herring fillets

250g oatmeal

½ tbsp vegetable or sunflower oil

Salt and pepper, to taste

1 lemon

Melt 100g of the butter in a saucepan or microwaveable bowl. Dip the herring fillets into the melted butter, so they are covered, then season with salt and pepper. Roll the herring in the oatmeal until fully coated, then set aside ready for frying.

Heat the oil in a frying pan and when the oil is warm, place the prepared herring fillets in the pan flesh side down. Cook for 2-3 minutes on each side until tender. Once the fish is cooked, remove it from the pan while you finish the dish.

Juice the lemon and melt the remaining 25g of butter in the pan used to cook the herring. Add the fresh lemon juice to the hot butter, mix together, and then spoon this simple sauce over the fried herring. Present your herring on the plate and enjoy.

PREPARATION TIME: 5 MINUTES | COOKING TIME: 10 MINUTES | SERVES 2

THE MARINE CONSERVATION SOCIETY'S GOOD FISH GUIDE

BY JACK CLARKE, SUSTAINABLE SEAFOOD ADVOCATE

"There are scores of delicious and sustainable options available right here on our coasts and the Good Fish Guide, along with brilliant books like this, are a great place to find inspiration."

At the Marine Conservation Society, we think sustainable fishing and fish farming are hugely important in delivering ocean-friendly food and jobs for people in all corners of the UK. We know it can be complicated trying to unpick and understand the latest science; that's why we launched the Good Fish Guide over 20 years ago.

Originally a book, these days it's a website, downloadable to your phone, offering the most up to date sustainability information for most of the seafood you can catch, buy, or eat in the UK. All you need to know is what species it is, where it was caught or farmed, and how it was caught or farmed. Pop this information into the Good Fish Guide and we can tell you whether it's a green-rated Best Choice, an OK amber or red-rated Fish to Avoid.

The sustainability of seafood can vary but we update our Good Fish Guide ratings twice every year so you can rest assured that they're accurate and reflect the latest science and environmental conditions. Because of the changeable nature of seafood, it's important to be flexible with your recipes too.

There are scores of delicious and sustainable options available right here on our coasts and the Good Fish Guide, along with brilliant books like this, are a great place to find inspiration. If a certain species isn't available at your local fishmonger, or has a poor rating, the Good Fish Guide will suggest more sustainable alternatives. Sometimes this will be the same fish from a more sustainable fishery or farm, or it may be a totally different fish, but with a similar flavour profile.

Farmed shellfish, like the mussels in our recipe, are an incredible future-proof superfood. Unlike most farmed animals, they don't need feeding or watering, and there are no chemicals or vaccines. They actively clean the environment they're raised in, with each mussel filtering around 40 litres of water every day. They can have even a lower impact on the planet than some farmed vegetables! An ocean-friendly treat that's also easy on your wallet, they are a great place to start when it comes to cooking and eating fish and seafood.

Photo © Sam Mansfield

Photo © Martin Stevens

Photo © Billy Barraclough

Photo © Mark Harris

© Harry Flook

Photo © Billy Barraclough

Photo © Phil Wilkinson

Photo © Billy Barraclough

Photo © Billy Barraclough

THAI RED CURRY MUSSELS

Mussels are a sustainable superfood, and this dish brings out their best. You probably already have some of the ingredients for this curry paste in your store cupboard; it's easy to make, and complements fresh mussels perfectly.

For the paste

½ lemongrass stalk, roughly chopped

1 kaffir lime leaf, torn and central stalk discarded

3 red chillies, deseeded and roughly chopped (leave the seeds in if you prefer more heat)

25g fresh coriander, leaves and stalks separated, roughly chopped

1 small shallot, roughly chopped

3 cloves of garlic, roughly chopped

½ tsp galangal paste

1 tsp ground white pepper

¼ tsp ground cumin

¼ tsp ground coriander

For the mussels

1kg fresh mussels

1 tsp sunflower oil

1 small onion, finely chopped

1 lemongrass stalk, bashed with a pestle

400ml coconut milk

1 red chilli, cut into fine rings for garnish

For the paste

Place the lemongrass into a mortar with a pinch of salt and pound to a paste. Add the kaffir lime leaf and repeat, then repeat with the chillies, coriander stems, shallot, and lastly the garlic. Mix in the galangal. Finally, stir in the white pepper, cumin and coriander. Set aside.

For the mussels

Thoroughly rinse the mussels under cold water and remove any beards. Discard any that are cracked or do not close during this process or when tapped. Set aside.

Heat the oil in a pan on a low-medium heat and cook the onion until soft and translucent, about 5-10 minutes. Increase the heat to medium, add the paste and lemongrass and cook while stirring for a minute. Add the coconut milk and cook for a further 2 minutes. Add the mussels, cover and simmer for 3-4 minutes, shaking the pan every so often, until they open.

Remove the lemongrass and discard any mussels that have not opened. Serve the mussels sprinkled with the chilli rings and chopped coriander leaves, with jasmine rice or crusty bread.

PREPARATION TIME: 35 MINUTES | COOKING TIME: 15 MINUTES | SERVES 2

NINTH WAVE RESTAURANT

BY CARLA LAMONT

"Over the last 14 years Jonny has played a Hebridean version of Clark Kent: by day he wears yellow oilskins and wellies on the high seas, then in a magical turnaround arrives for dinner service in his kilt and sporran outfit with all the trimmings."

I am the chef at Ninth Wave, a wee seafood and game restaurant on the wild moors of the Isle of Mull in the Hebrides. The restaurant was built out of a 200-year-old bothy which is on seven acres of wildflower croft and was lovingly renovated in 2009 by myself and the co-owner, my husband Jonny. We wanted to create a place that we would love to eat at, filled with all our favourite things: sumptuous surroundings, gorgeous décor, personable service, creative cocktails, unique dishes with a wow-factor, and comfortable chairs! Our dedication to this end has seen us proudly becoming multi-time winners of Scottish Restaurant of the Year and Best Dining Experience Scotland.

Our seafood comes in fresh daily from our own boat, the Sonsie. We enjoy using many sustainable by-catches such as octopus, sea urchin and conger eel as well as crab and lobster. Over the last 14 years Jonny has played a Hebridean version of Clark Kent: by day he wears yellow oilskins and wellies on the high seas, then in a magical turnaround arrives for dinner service in his kilt and sporran outfit with all the trimmings.

I am from the great melting pot of culture that is Canada's west coast. On our menu, you will find many dishes inspired by my homeland's ethnic cuisines. Jonny and I visit different countries on culinary tours each winter and bring back ingredients and ideas from our travels. Colourful spices from markets in Marrakesh, the street food of Baha Mexico and the coconut-laden dishes of Kerala have all appeared on our menu, using the very freshest Scottish produce. Our wee greenhouses boast kaffir lime, Meyer lemons, Vietnamese coriander, cardamom, turmeric, tomatillos and much more. We grow or catch 80% of our produce and our lovely diners say they can taste the difference!

The restaurant takes its name from Celtic mythology, in which "the land of other-worldly delights" starts at the ninth wave. This spirit is reflected in both Ninth Wave's eclectic style of cuisine and in an ethos where luxury meets sustainability.

Jonny retired from front of house in 2022, so changes are afoot. Instead of a night venue, we will be offering luxury four course lunches for meetings, parties, receptions and the newly emerging gastro-tour market. We are very excited to continue to evolve and offer diners the very best of Mull.

CRAB WAFFLES WITH MALTAISE MAYO

· ·

A deliciously moreish starter or brunch course. Our crab comes straight off our boat, the Sonsie, which can often be seen bobbing jauntily around the Sound of Iona waters with Jonny-fisherman at the helm. Classic flavours of tarragon and mandarin orange make this a fresh and vibrant dish.

For the Maltaise mayo

120ml mayonnaise

1 tbsp fresh lemon juice

1 tbsp + 1 tsp fresh mandarin juice

½ tsp grated mandarin orange zest

½ tsp finely chopped fresh tarragon

Pinch of freshly ground white pepper

Salt, to taste

For the crab waffles

2 large eggs

2 spring onions, thinly sliced

200g fresh white crabmeat, (or tinned, drained and squeezed dry)

120g panko breadcrumbs

85g fresh or tinned sweetcorn, drained and patted dry

80ml mayonnaise

10ml chopped fresh dill

¼ tsp dry mustard

¼ tsp salt

Ground black pepper, to taste

Spray cooking oil

For the garnish

60g fresh white crab meat

Micro greens

Primroses, pansies or other edible flowers

Preheat your waffle maker as per the instructions.

Make the Maltaise mayo by mixing all the ingredients together in a bowl with a whisk.

To make the crab waffles, first whisk the eggs in a large bowl until frothy. Stir in all the remaining ingredients, then shape the mixture into 4 cakes the shape of your waffle grid (usually about 10cm square and 1.5cm thick).

Spray your waffle maker with cooking oil and place one portion of the crab mix in each section of the waffle maker. Cook for 5 minutes or until well browned, as per the machine's instructions.

Meanwhile, warm 4 plates ready to serve the waffles. Place two diagonally cut halves of the crab waffle piled one atop the other and offset. Garnish with the remaining crab meat in a decorative dollop and drizzle with your Maltaise mayo. Finish off with micro greens and edible flowers such as pansies or primroses.

OFFSHORE SHELLFISH LTD.

BY SARAH HOLMYARD, HEAD OF SALES AND MARKETING

"Our methods are based on years of research and trials, and we have worked with world-leading marine scientists from Plymouth University to study the ecological and environmental benefits that mussel farming at scale in offshore waters brings, proving beyond doubt the benefits of low-trophic aquaculture."

We are a family-run, sustainable, rope-grown mussel farm based in beautiful Lyme Bay, South Devon, where we farm offshore in the open ocean, between three and six miles out to sea. John Holmyard is our founder and, following a degree in marine biology, has been farming mussels for 35 years. Family members Nicki, Sarah and George all play important roles within the business, keeping everything running smoothly both onshore and offshore.

We are pioneers of the offshore mussel industry in the UK and have created our own unique and truly sustainable way to farm mussels in the open ocean. By developing these new methods, we have opened up a previously inaccessible area to grow our sustainable crop. Baby mussels (spat) settle naturally on the ropes we suspend beneath buoyed headlines in the water in late spring each year. We thin out the lines a few months later and return the mussel seed to the sea using biodegradable cotton socking, through which the growing rope is passed. From spat to harvest takes just over one year. Our farm also creates a habitat for many other species, as the mussel lines provide a nursery for juvenile crabs, shrimp, scallops and more to grow.

The mussels we produce have consistently high meat yields and clean, large shells due to the low-density way in which we farm. The headlines are spaced far apart, to ensure that the mussels have ample access to the natural nutrients and phytoplankton on which they feed. Our methods are based on years of research and trials, and we have worked with world-leading marine scientists from Plymouth University to study the ecological and environmental benefits that mussel farming at scale in offshore waters brings, proving beyond doubt the benefits of low-trophic aquaculture.

Our farm is a huge achievement in terms of responsible future food production, and we are proud to have gained three globally recognised accreditations from the Aquaculture Stewardship Council, Best Aquaculture Practices, and Soil Association Organic. Sustainability and the creation of a high-quality product that benefits the environment are key to what we set out to achieve.

Working in a thriving marine environment and seeing the wonderful life and growth in the area make the work that we do, and the long, hard days at sea, very worthwhile. We look forward to seeing the farm continue to grow and develop.

MUSSEL & POTATO SOUP

Enjoy this simple, tasty, seafood winter warmer, which combines mussels, potatoes, onions, milk and cream to make a hearty meal.

1kg fresh mussels

200g potatoes

2 shallots

2 cloves of garlic

20ml olive oil

Black pepper

400ml milk

50ml single cream

Small bunch of fresh parsley (optional)

Rinse the mussels and remove the beards, then put in a pan with 2 tablespoons of water. Discard any mussels that do not close when sharply tapped on a hard surface. Cook on a high heat, with the lid on the pan, for 4-5 minutes, until all the shells are open. Drain the mussels, retaining the juice. Leave to cool slightly, then remove the meat from the shells.

Meanwhile, make the mussel juice up to 400ml with water. Dice the potatoes into 2cm cubes, finely dice the shallots and crush the garlic cloves.

Heat the olive oil in a pan and gently sweat the shallots and garlic without browning them. Add the diced potatoes to the pan, followed by your mussel stock. Season the mixture with plenty of black pepper. The mussel juice will be quite salty, so do not add salt until the soup is cooked as it may not be needed.

Bring back to simmering point, then cook for 10 minutes until the potatoes are soft. Using a handheld masher, break up the potatoes slightly to thicken the soup.

Add the mussel meat, milk and cream to the pan and bring the soup back to a simmer. Serve with chopped parsley and crusty bread.

PREPARATION TIME: 20 MINUTES | COOKING TIME: 30 MINUTES | SERVES 4

ORKNEY FISHERIES ASSOCIATION

BY HANNAH FENNELL

"The Orkney Fisheries Association was set up 50 years ago by Orcadian fishermen who wanted to represent the interests of Orkney's fishing industry, promote sustainable fishing practices, and help improve knowledge of the marine environment and the species within it."

For many fishermen, fishing is much more than a job — it is a way of life, providing fishers with a sense of satisfaction, a connection to the environment and, ultimately, with an identity and a community that spans across the globe. The Orkney Islands is a small archipelago located off the north coast of Scotland, with an inshore fishing fleet of over 100 boats, the majority of which are under 10m in length. Lobsters and brown and velvet crabs are the most valuable species to the fishery, and this is reflected in the presence of two crab-processing factories on the islands.

The Orkney Fisheries Association was set up 50 years ago by Orcadian fishermen who wanted to represent the interests of Orkney's fishing industry, promote sustainable fishing practices, and help improve knowledge of the marine environment and the species within it. Since its establishment, members of Orkney Fisheries Association have worked hard to make sure our fishing is as sustainable and low impact as possible.

One of the most successful projects undertaken by the islands' fishermen is the V Notch Lobster, to allow egg-bearing female lobsters to mature. If an egg-bearing lobster is caught the fishermen will cut a V shape into its tail before releasing it back into the sea. This allows the eggs to have a chance of survival and ensures the industry remains sustainable. The notch will last for four years and during that time it is illegal to land or sell a lobster with this mark. Larger females will also produce more eggs.

Another project is scallop tagging which aims to understand and explore the movements of scallops. Launched in 2012, the project designed by fishermen was the first of its kind and demonstrated that within a month, half of the scallops in a given area would move, with new entrants coming in to replace them. Undersized scallops are tagged before being released back into the sea. When they are caught again the numbering system on the tag will help to chart how far they have travelled.

CRAB SOUP

A twist on a traditional Orcadian recipe for crab soup, this dish is an excellent winter warmer.

30g butter

1 large onion

1 carrot

1 stick of celery

55g rice

300ml fish stock (can also use chicken stock)

600ml milk

225g crabmeat (white and brown)

30ml Thai fish sauce

Salt and black pepper, to taste

Chopped fresh parsley, for garnish

Melt the butter in a large saucepan while you peel and chop the onion, carrot and celery.

Add the vegetables to the pan and cook for 3-4 minutes to soften slightly. Stir in the rice and cook for another 1-2 minutes.

Add the fish stock and milk, then bring to the boil. Reduce the heat and simmer the mixture for 15-20 minutes or until the rice and vegetables are cooked.

Purée the soup in a liquidiser or blender. Return it to the pan and then stir in the crabmeat and fish sauce. Heat gently for about 5 minutes, then taste and adjust the seasoning with salt and pepper as needed. Serve the soup sprinkled with chopped parsley.

OSBORNE & SONS (SHELLFISH) LIMITED

BY GRAHAM OSBORNE

"We believe in supplying and producing the best products and dishes to our customers, whether that is traditional shellfish such as cockles and jellied eels or creating inspiring dishes with them such as our cockles and fries."

We have long been associated with the fishing industry in Leigh-on-Sea, an historic fishing town on the banks of the Thames Estuary. Our business dates back over 140 years, spanning five generations of the Osborne family all the way to us: Graham Osborne and Andrew Lawrence. We are immensely proud of our heritage, where it all began, and the story so far, one that we continue to write.

Our business has been built on cockling, an industry that has seen much change over the last 100 years. We fish our cockles from the Thames Estuary fishery, which was awarded MSC accreditation several years ago. Our commitment to the industry has seen us invest in new cooking machinery in our factory in the Old Town and more recently we have built a state-of-the-art IQF factory to tap into new markets for our products.

At the heart of what we do is the desire to produce a high yielding, plump, sweet cockle for our customers near and far to enjoy. We are well known within the shellfish industry for this and have been the recipient of several awards – including Great Taste Awards 2022 and Great British Food Awards (Seafood) 2021 and 2022 – which recognise this.

Our retail presence in our local area is prominent, with our business sitting in the heart of Old Leigh where we have our café and fishmongers for people to buy and enjoy our products whilst watching the fishing boats go by.

We have opened a second fishmongers within the town, and part of this story is our Seafood School where we run courses for both adults and children to gain confidence in choosing, preparing and cooking seafood, from filleting fish, creating dinner party dishes, and cooking seasonally to learning about our trusted seafood suppliers.

Our commitment, passion and intrinsic link to Leigh-on-Sea and the cockle industry drives us forward and remains at the heart of what we do.

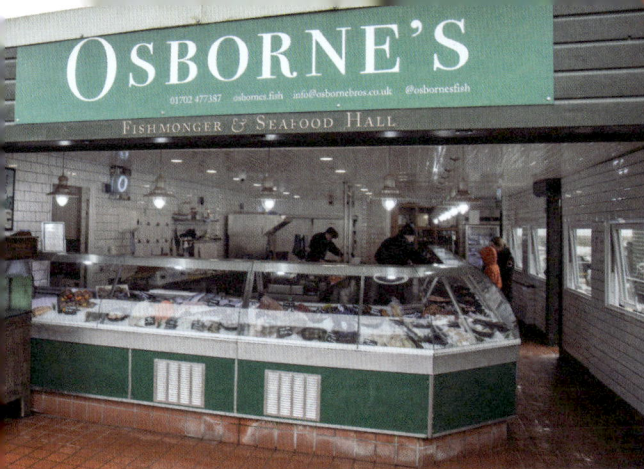

COCKLE & BACON CHOWDER

There is only one main ingredient that we could use in our dish and that is our Leigh-on-Sea cockles! We've paired them with classic ingredients to make a velvety winter warming chowder, served with beautiful fresh bread. We often serve it inside a hollowed-out cob from our local bakery.

50g butter

150g unsmoked bacon lardons, cubed pancetta or chopped streaky bacon

1 onion, finely chopped

Sprig of thyme

1 bay leaf

35g plain flour

800ml fish stock

150ml milk

150ml double cream

2 medium potatoes, cubed (about 250g)

300g Osborne's cooked cockles

Salt and black pepper

Heat the butter in a pan and sizzle the bacon for 3-4 minutes until it starts to brown. Stir in the onion, thyme and bay and cook everything gently for 10 minutes until the onion is soft and golden. Scatter over the flour and stir in to make a sandy paste, cook for a further 2 minutes, then gradually stir in the fish stock, followed by the milk and cream.

Add the potatoes, bring everything to a simmer and leave to bubble away gently for 10 minutes or until the potatoes are cooked. Use a fork to crush a few of the potato chunks against the side of the pan to help thicken the chowder – you still want lots of defined chunks though.

Stir through the cockle meat and simmer for a minute to reheat. Season with plenty of black pepper and a little salt, if needed.

Serve with a fresh cob loaf, cut into wedges, or if you are feeling indulgent, hollow out a fresh cob loaf (you can use the bread for breadcrumbs at a later point) and use this as your serving bowl.

PADSTOW BOATYARD

BY JONATHAN GOODE-CROWE

"Employing skilled boat builders, carpenters, laminators and engineers from the local area, Padstow Boatyard has become part of Padstow's lifeblood, with traditional fishing boats coming up and down the slipway for refit and repairs."

Padstow Boatyard is the trading name of Claxton Composites Ltd, set up by Will Claxton and incorporated in 2013. The company started off humbly with a few guys repairing and building racing yachts and providing short-term composite laminating labour for bespoke boat build projects. During the construction of a vessel at the boatyard in Padstow, the company saw an opportunity to take on permanent premises and move its wealth of knowledge and experience with custom fibreglass boat building from racing yachts into commercial fishing boats, so Padstow Boatyard was born.

Employing skilled boat builders, carpenters, laminators and engineers from the local area, Padstow Boatyard has become part of Padstow's lifeblood, with traditional fishing boats coming up and down the slipway for refit and repairs. The large commercial premises operate at all hours while tourists meander around the harbour to experience the fresh local seafood and watch as the fishermen arrive back with their catch.

The company has built numerous custom designed GRP commercial fishing vessels for fishermen in the UK and overseas as well as refitting and repairing commercial fishing, survey and passenger vessels for a range of customers from all around. We cultivate good working relationships with key suppliers and design partners, staying local wherever possible to create the most fuel-efficient, economic and practical custom-designed vessels possible.

The scope of work that the boatyard carries out has also broadened across several sectors, but it remains one of the only boatyards in the UK to have the pioneering skills and experience to build such large commercial fishing vessels to full sail-away stage in GRP. We have found the demand for high quality, innovatively designed commercial fishing boats has increased significantly, both in the UK and emerging markets overseas.

Over the last few years, Padstow Boatyard has invested heavily in modern production facilities, equipment and recruitment. As a result, the workforce has increased to include more skilled boat builders and laminators as well as a business manager. Our facilities include a 150-tonne capacity build facility with 10t crane, office, 150ft quayside and slipway with hauling winch and cradle to pull vessels into the covered work shed area.

Our future aim is to enhance our product and service offering so we can provide the next generation of commercial fishing and leisure vessels; we want to be an integral part of the UK boat building industry for many years to come, keeping Padstow firmly on the map where it belongs.

STARGAZY PIE
BY THE CORNISH FISHMONGER

Perhaps the most famous (and strangest) of all Cornish fish dishes... Originating from Mousehole, it is traditionally eaten during Tom Bawcock's Eve on December 23rd in honour of the famous fisherman. Legend has it he braved the elements during a wild and stormy winter, getting a catch so large he saved the village from starvation.

20ml vegetable oil

1 large fennel bulb, finely chopped

1 clove of garlic, peeled and chopped

2 fresh tomatoes, finely diced

1 tsp ground turmeric

1 tsp ground coriander

1 tsp ground cumin

Pinch of Cornish sea salt

400g hake fillets or other Cornish fish, diced

6 whole sardines, gutted

100g ready-rolled shortcrust pastry

1 egg, beaten

Preheat the oven to 180°c. Heat a frying pan, add the vegetable oil and soften the fennel, garlic and tomatoes with the spices and sea salt.

Meanwhile, neatly arrange the diced fish in a pie dish. Spread the fennel and tomato mixture evenly over the top, then lay the sardines on the mixture with their heads facing skywards.

Cut the shortcrust pastry to size so it fits the pie dish and then cover the filling to make a lid, leaving the heads of the sardines poking out of the pastry. Seal the edges and brush the top with the beaten egg.

Bake your pie in the preheated oven for 20-30 minutes, then serve hot with lots of dressed salad leaves and buttered potatoes.

PREPARATION TIME: 20 MINUTES | COOKING TIME: 20 MINUTES | SERVES 4-6

ROCKFISH

BY MITCH TONKS

"It is important to me that we can enjoy seafood now and well into the future, which is why sustainability is so important at Rockfish. We only buy from boats we know and trust and I'm constantly travelling to find the most sustainable fisheries in the world so we can learn from them."

I grew up by the sea in Weston-super-Mare, and one of my earliest memories is of cooking seafood with my grandmother. We would head off to our local fishmonger and choose from shrimp, crab, gurnard and dab, then go home to pick the crab, peel the shrimp and prepare the fish. Little did I know that this would set fire to what has become a lifelong passion for seafood.

I opened my first fishmongers in Bath in 1996 so I could indulge that passion and share it with people. Fishmongers had become quite stale at that time, and I wanted to put the excitement back. It naturally followed that I wanted to cook fish so, armed with Elizabeth David and Jane Grigson books, I taught myself to cook and opened a restaurant called the Green Street Seafood Café. It became quite a hit and took me on a journey that ended up by the sea again in Dartmouth, where we opened The Seahorse and founded Rockfish.

We now have nine restaurants, but the core belief remains the same: to help more people enjoy delicious, sustainable seafood. Rockfish has a unique supply chain and way of working which all stems from our base at the Brixham quayside, right next to the UK's biggest fish market. Every day our experienced team walk the market and select the fish from the boats we know and trust. We also have our own boat, The Rockfisher, who fishes for local seafood from Brixham. The fish we buy is prepared and portioned by our expert fishmongers right at the quayside, then sent to our restaurants and directly to people's homes through our online seafood market that same day.

It is important to me that we can enjoy seafood now and well into the future, which is why sustainability is so important at Rockfish. We only buy from boats we know and trust and I'm constantly travelling to find the most sustainable fisheries in the world so we can learn from them. When fish is in abundance, we buy it and blast freeze it at the quayside so people can enjoy that fish at its best, even if the boats can't go out. We also preserve British-landed fish like mackerel, mussels and cuttlefish in peak condition for our range of Rockfish tinned seafood, allowing people to enjoy this delicious healthy food all year round.

MACKEREL SHAWARMA

···

I love the flavours of a good kebab so here they are with one of my favourite fish. This really is a flavour explosion. There's lots going on, from the smokiness of the mackerel to the garlic yoghurt, fresh herbs and crunchy salad.

75g white cabbage, finely sliced

1 lemon, juiced

1 mackerel, filleted and skinned

1 heaped tbsp plain flour

Pinch of ground cloves

Pinch of ground cardamom

Pinch of ground cinnamon

Pinch of white pepper

Olive oil, for frying

2 flour tortillas

1 tomato, chopped

½ small red onion, finely sliced root to top

Small bunch of dill, chopped

Pinch of za'atar (a Lebanese spice sold in most supermarkets)

1 fresh green chilli, finely sliced

Pinch of chilli flakes

2 tbsp pomegranate seeds

For the smoked mackerel hummus

1 smoked mackerel fillet, skinned

80g tinned chickpeas, rinsed and drained

1 tbsp tahini

2 tbsp mayonnaise

½ lemon, zested

For the garlic yoghurt

1 clove of garlic, crushed

2 tbsp plain yoghurt

To make the hummus, combine the smoked mackerel, chickpeas and tahini in a food processor and blitz to a smooth paste. Transfer to a bowl, then fold in the mayonnaise and lemon zest. Set aside until ready to serve. To make the garlic yoghurt, mix the ingredients together with a good pinch of salt. Now dress the sliced cabbage with the fresh lemon juice and set aside.

Remove any pin bones from the mackerel fillets. Mix the flour with the cloves, cardamom, cinnamon and pepper, then dip the mackerel fillets in this mixture to coat both sides. Fry in a little olive oil, skinned side down, for about 2 minutes or until crisp. Turn over and finish cooking on the other side for about 1 minute. Leave the mackerel in the pan, off the heat, while you assemble the wraps.

Warm the tortillas, then lay them out and spread the smoked mackerel hummus over them. Scatter over the cabbage, then the tomato and onion followed by plenty of dill. Lay a mackerel fillet on each tortilla. Add a tablespoon of garlic yoghurt, then sprinkle liberally with za'atar, fresh chilli, chilli flakes and pomegranate seeds. Fold the bottom in and wrap it all up to serve.

ROSSMORE OYSTERS LTD.

BY TRISTAN HUGH-JONES

"There's nothing I enjoy more than being out on the boat on a bright sunny morning, having my working day dictated by the tides rather than anything else, and just being part of the cycle of growing and nurturing our baby oysters..."

Oysters have been part of my life for ever. My father David started the business in 1969, when he and my mother Bridget set off, newly married, to Ireland in their old transit van and settled into Rossmore, near Cork. The house and buildings were a near-derelict farmstead but there was an incredible body of water beside it: a sheltered estuary with warm, shallow water and a lovely firm bottom. It's a unique eco-system that's been a natural home for oysters since Neolithic times, and we still find the occasional huge oyster midden tucked along the shores.

I was born on the oyster farm in 1973, was helping my father dredge oysters by the age of seven, and have had a passion for oysters ever since. There's nothing I enjoy more than being out on the boat on a bright sunny morning, having my working day dictated by the tides rather than anything else, and just being part of the cycle of growing and nurturing our baby oysters (or spat) from being almost invisible, only millimetres long, to something we can sell to top restaurants after a few years.

We've established a successful breeding programme, where we grow our native oysters in 21 man-made (or Dad-made) ponds. We scatter mussel shells which cover the side and floor of the ponds and the oyster larve grow there for a few months, before scooping them all out and scattering them in carefully defined beds in the estuary, where they grow for another four years. It's hard, physical work, and can sometimes be quite monotonous, but there's always some quirk of tide or weather that makes it different.

The business has expanded to include a depot in London, where we have large holding tanks and can grade, clean and pack oysters for the London market. We also farm the last native oyster bed in Loch Ryan, Scotland. The combination of Brexit and Covid have made the last few years a nightmare thanks to plummeting demand and disastrous paperwork requirements, but I'm determined to keep the farm going from strength to strength. If there's one thing my father has taught me, it's that fortune favours the brave! My role now is more office-based; I run the distribution as well as handling sales. I've got a great team around me: Rab and John in Loch Ryan; Neil, Chris, Debbie and Karen in London; and my brother Rupert who runs the farm in Cork. I would be absolutely lost without them.

CHAMPAGNE OYSTERS

My wife Vickie loves cooked oysters (more than just slurping them straight from the sea) and whilst visiting her sister-in-law in Shanagarry, County Cork, found this was a delightful way to consume oysters with very little stress, for great enjoyment.

18 large native oysters

2 shallots, finely chopped

1 bottle of Champagne

½ pint of double cream

Black pepper, to taste

Place the finely chopped shallots and champagne in a pan on a medium heat. Simmer until the liquid has reduced to about a third of the original volume.

Add the cream and any oyster juices with a little black pepper, then continue to simmer until the sauce has reduced to about half a pint in total.

Preheat the grill and open the oysters so the meat is completely detached, then place the oysters in their cupped shells on the grill tray.

Divide the sauce between the oysters and place under the grill on a high heat for 3-4 minutes until the sauce bubbles and turns golden brown.

Allow the oysters to cool slightly and then serve immediately!

PREPARATION TIME: 40 MINUTES | COOKING TIME: 3-4 MINUTES | SERVES 6

SCOTT'S RESTAURANT

· ·

BY TOM FRASER

"The world of fish and seafood is so versatile as every species lends itself to different accompaniments, cooking techniques, flavours and textures. In the restaurant kitchen, I love the fact that this means we'll have loads going on at once: shellfish on a Plancha plate, fish poaching, a whole seabass on the charcoal grill..."

I properly discovered fish and seafood when I started working at Scott's Restaurant in Mayfair and have stuck with it throughout my career ever since. Today, I'm the head chef of Scott's Richmond, a fish and seafood restaurant on the banks of the River Thames. We have an extensive menu featuring everything from caviar to cod: four different types of oysters and all the shellfish you would expect, classic fish dishes and daily specials that depend on what's available whether that's razor clams or Scottish langoustines. We also like to make sure some of the options are new and exciting, like our scallops in XO sauce and octopus carpaccio.

I want Scott's to be a seafood restaurant that people know they can come to for the best produce around. Our suppliers play a big part in this; we source mainly from dayboats including the Wright Brothers in Brixham, phoning round each morning to find out what everyone has landed for the best quality and price. Part of what I enjoy about working with fish and seafood as a chef is the precision it can require; the fine margins for cooking it well are a great challenge. It also ties into one of my hobbies, sea fishing: I love going down to parts of the British coastline like Lyme Regis in the summer to cast off the rocks and see what I can catch, like wild bass, dabs, plaice, mackerel and more.

The world of fish and seafood is so versatile as every species lends itself to different accompaniments, cooking techniques, flavours and textures. In the restaurant kitchen, I love the fact that this means we'll have loads going on at once: shellfish on a Plancha plate, fish poaching, a whole seabass on the charcoal grill… I also cook regularly at home as there's nothing better than fresh lobster or scallops on the barbecue. My wife is also a chef and we get our kids involved where we can. I think people would maybe be more receptive to cooking and eating seafood if we can find more original ways of treating fish. For example, if people come to Scott's and aren't keen on oysters, we suggest they try the tempura oyster first – because who doesn't like deep fried food in crispy batter! – which often acts as a gateway to other seafood they haven't tried before.

PAN FRIED CHALK STREAM TROUT WITH CLAMS, COCKLES AND TROUT ROE BUTTER SAUCE

Before cooking this delicious dish, you'll need to make sure the trout portions are nice and dry to get a crisp skin when pan frying. The cockles and clams will also need to be purged, which means soaking them in salt water to remove any sand that may be trapped inside them.

4 x 160g skin-on chalk stream trout portions (salmon or sea trout will do)

200g cockles

200g surf clams

80ml white wine

1 banana shallot, peeled and finely sliced

1 sprig of tarragon

5 white peppercorns

20ml white wine vinegar

40ml double cream

200g cold butter, diced

1 lemon

Salt and pepper

Handful of sea herbs, lightly blanched (sea aster, sea purslane or sea beets)

½ bunch of chives, finely chopped

50g trout roe

Olive oil

If necessary, lay the trout portions skin side down on a cloth or kitchen paper in the fridge for an hour or so before cooking, to ensure they are dry. Meanwhile, inspect the cockles and clams, discarding any that are broken. The shells should feel heavy and be tightly closed. Place them in a bowl, just cover with cold salted water and leave for 30 minutes. Drain and rinse the shellfish thoroughly under cold running water in a colander, shaking vigorously to remove further sediment.

Place a pan on a medium-high heat. Add the cleaned cockles and clams with half of the white wine and cover with a lid. Cook until they have all fully opened, then transfer the shellfish to a bowl with a slotted spoon. Once the liquid in the pan has settled, carefully remove two tablespoons from the top, leaving any sediment behind. Remove three quarters of the cockles and clams from their shells, leaving the rest in for presentation.

To make the butter sauce, place the shallot, tarragon, peppercorns, vinegar, and remaining wine in a clean saucepan with the reserved cooking liquid. Reduce until you have around 4 tablespoons of liquid left, then add the double cream and reduce again to around 4 tablespoons. Turn down to a gentle heat and gradually whisk in the cold butter until you have a thick, buttery sauce. Pass this through a sieve into another pan, then season with salt and pepper and add a squeeze of lemon juice to taste. Cover the pan and keep at an ambient temperature until needed.

To cook the trout, put a wide non-stick frying pan on a medium heat. Season the trout with salt and pepper and place the portions skin side down into the pan. Cook for 3-4 minutes. Meanwhile, gently reheat the butter sauce (but do not let it boil) and then add the cockles and clams. Heat for 1 minute, then add the sea herbs, chopped chives and trout roe.

By this time, you should see the colour of the trout changing as the fish cooks. Once the trout portions have cooked halfway through, turn them over and cook for a further 2 minutes. Remove from the pan and place into serving bowls. The skin should be nice and crisp, and the trout should still be blushing pink in the middle. Equally divide the cockles and clams between the bowls and generously spoon over the butter sauce. Finish with a drizzle of olive oil.

SEA HAZE

BY JACK MESSENGER

"At Sea Haze we are passionate about trying to get more people and restaurants to eat more local fish, as over half our UK fish goes to export. It's caught here and then flown all around the world because we eat so little fish in the UK compared to the rest of Europe, but we want to change that."

Our fresh fish shop was established in 1995 by my dad's uncle, Alan, and my dad then took over the shop in 2002. I started learning to take over Sea Haze when I was 15 years old, back in 2012, as I had always wanted to get involved with the family business. My dad Neil has taught me everything I know, from how to fillet fish to running the shop. He also goes out fishing day and night, as most of what we sell at Sea Haze is caught by our family on a 32-foot day boat from Brighton's seafront.

I think Sea Haze is a very special shop, as no one else has tried catching and selling their own fish on Brighton seafront for years. You won't get anything fresher than what we can offer our customers; sometimes people will be having fish for dinner that is less than 6 or 7 hours old. One thing I learnt from customers is that the reason people stay clear of fish is because they hate the bones, but I can always guarantee that if you buy fillets of fish from Sea Haze, there won't be a bone in sight.

At Sea Haze we are passionate about trying to get more people and restaurants to eat more local fish, as over half our UK fish goes to export. It's caught here and then flown all around the world because we eat so little fish in the UK compared to the rest of Europe, but we want to change that.

One of my proudest moments within the family business was winning the Bite Sussex Fish & Seafood Rising Star Award in 2021. Following that, a local newspaper called The Argus got in touch and published an article about me, the shop and the fishing industry. The shop has transformed in the last ten years since I joined the business and has a great reputation throughout Brighton and Sussex. Alongside the fresh fish and seafood that my dad brings in on our boat, my nan Jacky is a big part of the reason that Sea Haze has so many returning customers. She used to run a shop of her own years ago and would teach me all about customer service, so I have her to thank for all our regulars.

PAN-FRIED SUSSEX TURBOT

This recipe by one of Jack's regular customers, Jessie Kay Stanbrook, uses a flavoursome local fish served with local clams, samphire and buttered potatoes for a delicious yet quick and easy dinner.

300g live clams, cleaned (see method)

500g baby potatoes (or a waxy variety, such as Charlotte), halved or quartered depending on size

2 fillets of turbot (between 200-300g each)

4 tbsp unsalted butter

2 shallots, finely chopped

1 lemon, half zested

1-2 cloves of garlic, minced

Pinch of chilli flakes

Handful of fresh tarragon, leaves pulled off the stalk (approx. 20 small leaves)

200ml dry white wine or vermouth

150g samphire, rinsed

First, rinse the clams in a colander a few times and then submerge them in heavily salted water for 2 hours. Rinse again once ready to use.

Wash the potatoes and then boil them with the skins on in salted water until a fork goes through easily. This takes around 10-15 minutes depending on their size. Once done, drain and put back in the pan with the lid on to keep warm.

While the potatoes cook, dry the turbot fillets with a paper towel, then generously season both sides with salt and pepper. Put 3 tablespoons of the butter in a wide pan with a lid on a medium heat. Once the pan is hot and the butter has melted, place the turbot fillets in skin side down and cook for approximately 2-3 minutes. Carefully turn the turbot over and cook for another 1-1.5 minutes. If the fish is sticking to the pan when you try and turn it, leave it for another 30 seconds or so and it should 'cook' off. When the turbot flesh is white all the way through, carefully lift the fillets out the pan and place them on a hot plate, then cover with foil.

Using the same pan, cook the chopped shallot for around a minute until soft, then add the lemon zest, garlic, chilli flakes and tarragon leaves to cook for another minute.

Add the wine to the shallot mixture, making sure to scrape anything that is stuck to the bottom of the pan. When you see bubbles in the sauce, throw in the cleaned clams and put the lid on to steam them for 3-4 minutes, shaking the pan every minute or so.

While the clams are steaming, heat the remaining butter in another frying pan. Gently fry the samphire for 3-4 minutes until soft and cooked through (it should still have a bite). Squeeze half the lemon over the samphire once it has been cooked but do not add salt, as it is already salty.

Check all the clams have opened (if not, steam them for another 30 seconds or so), then squeeze the other half of the lemon over them. Plate the turbot on hot plates, then place the clams on top and the samphire to the side.

Drop the boiled potatoes into the clam pan to reheat and coat them with the sauce, then divide between the plates. Cover the rest of the plates with the remaining sauce, then serve with extra wedges of lemon and enjoy!

PREPARATION TIME: 2 HOURS 30 MINUTES (INCLUDING WAITING TIME) | COOKING TIME: 25-30 MINUTES | SERVES 2

SEA MARIE

BY MARIE BUCHANAN

"The feeling I get from surfing a wave, being at one with the sea and the wind, completely absorbed in the moment without a care in the world, is what drives my passion and makes it all worthwhile."

I am a lifelong thalassophile: born by the sea, living for the sea, happiest when I'm at one with the sea! I have travelled the world competing internationally, initially as a windsurfer and latterly as a stand-up paddleboarder (SUP) where I became the most successful GB SUP athlete in September 2022, winning gold and silver medals at the ICF World Championships.

I was born in Devon with the sea in my blood: as a family we swam, fished, went rock pooling and shrimping, surfed and sailed, spending weekends and holidays aboard our sailing boat. In 2007, I achieved my dream of moving back to South Devon and while settling into my physiotherapy career, I was introduced to and quickly fell in love with the new sport of stand-up paddleboarding (SUP). I found SUP the perfect way to explore all the nooks and crannies in and around our beautiful South Hams coastline, getting up close to sea life and revisiting all the places we enjoyed as a family.

The beauty of SUP is its variety and simplicity; from flat water to fitness and even fishing, the possibilities are endless! The feeling I get from surfing a wave, being at one with the sea and the wind, completely absorbed in the moment without a care in the world, is what drives my passion and makes it all worthwhile. I also love to share my knowledge and skills with others, so in 2022 I set up my coaching and fitness business, Sea Marie, which combines my water skills with Pilates and physiotherapy. As a coach, there is nothing more satisfying than helping someone gain skills and fitness on the sea and watch their confidence and enjoyment grow.

In 2020 I met my partner Mark, a local fisherman, lifeboat coxswain, ocean sailor and not so average accountant! We soon discovered that we both lived for the sea. I jumped at the chance to join him aboard his 6.4 metre day boat, Minnehaha II, and learn all about his lobster fishing business. I absolutely love the simplicity and physical nature of this type of traditional and sustainable small-scale commercial fishing and enjoying the sea from a different perspective. Hope Cove supports four commercial fishermen, and the quality of the catch is exceptional. Weather limits days at sea, making this a naturally sustainable fishery. There's nothing more special or rewarding than enjoying eating your fresh catch within hours of landing!

© SupJunkie

FRESH LOBSTER WITH ZESTY MANGO SALSA

·······································

We're fortunate enough to catch our own lobsters, so they're often cooked within an hour of landing. Always use a fresh live lobster and not a frozen one, ideally bought direct from a registered fisherman or a specialist fishmonger, such as Catch of the Day in Kingsbridge.

1 live lobster (600g-750g)

1 mango

½ red onion

½ red pepper

½ cucumber

1 fresh red chilli

4 medium vine tomatoes

1-2 fresh limes, to taste

Olive oil

Handful of fresh mint leaves

Handful of fresh coriander (optional)

Salt and pepper, to taste

250g new potatoes

Mayonnaise (homemade if you choose!)

Fresh chives

50g butter

½ lemon, juiced

Salad of your choice, to serve

Rinse your lobster in cold water and then place in the freezer. This numbs them before cooking and, in our experience, is less distressing than killing with a knife, provided the water is on a rolling boil.

To prepare the mango salsa, dice the mango, onion, pepper, cucumber, and chilli into small cubes no bigger than the size of a pea. Remove the skins and seeds from the vine tomatoes and dice the flesh to the same size, then mix all the prepared ingredients together in a bowl. Stir in the lime juice and a drizzle of olive oil to marinate. Finely chop the mint and coriander, then fold the herbs into the salsa, adding salt and pepper to taste. Place the bowl in the fridge to chill until serving.

Rinse the new potatoes and cut to your preferred size if required, then place in a pan of boiling water and cook until al dente (approximately 10 minutes). Drain, leave to cool and then dress with mayonnaise and chives. Place the butter and lemon juice in a small bowl over a pan of hot water and leave to melt, stirring before serving.

Prepare a large pan of boiling water with a little salt for cooking the lobster. It's vital that this pan is large enough for the lobster to be completely immersed in boiling water so it dies instantly. If you don't have a pan large enough, kill your lobster first. When the water is at a rolling boil, remove the bands from the lobster's claws with a sharp knife and plunge it, head first, into boiling water. Put the lid on and boil for 12 minutes (do not overcook). Meanwhile, prepare a sink or large bowl of iced water. When the lobster is cooked, plunge it into cold water to stop the cooking process.

When cool enough to handle, remove the lobster from the water. Pull off and discard the head, then pull off the large claws by twisting to break them apart at each joint. Place each claw under a tea towel and hit with the back of a large knife to crack the shell. Stretch the lobster tail out on chopping board (it should want to spring shut) and halve it lengthways.

Plate the lobster, salsa and lemon butter to serve. This is my favourite way to eat our freshly caught lobsters and a great way to end a day's fishing – we hope you love it too!

THE SHOREHOUSE SEAFOOD RESTAURANT

BY JACKIE PEARCE

"It can be challenging and relentless; there would be weeks when we couldn't get out to sea due to the gales. Being totally dependent on the weather is probably the most trying aspect of making a living from the sea, but it's part of it and it's all we've known."

I always wanted to be a nurse when I grew up and never thought that I would be running a seasonal seafood restaurant on the west coast of Scotland. We bought The Shorehouse from my mother-in-law in May 1994. She set up the restaurant in 1978, which began with just three tables in what is now our living room. Back then it served open crab sandwiches, and today our best-selling item on the menu has always been the crab salad: simple but very popular.

I moved to the area in 1983 when I met my husband, who was then working at the local fish farm. After we had our first child, we decided to become self-employed and bought our first boat to run wildlife cruises. Several years later, we sold the Tystie and bought the Fulmar, which my husband and son still operate. They provide all our shellfish for The Shorehouse, which is landed at the pier right in front of the restaurant.

I've done my time on our boat too, working as the deckhand in the winter months. It can be challenging and relentless; there would be weeks when we couldn't get out to sea due to the gales. Being totally dependent on the weather is probably the most trying aspect of making a living from the sea, but it's part of it and it's all we've known. We've developed an alternative Christmas tradition, which involves the whole family (and any willing helpers) sizing velvet crabs a few days before Christmas. We would do this in all the weathers, drinking cup-a-soups and listening to Marshmallow World by Johnny Mathis! At the time, it was one of 'those' jobs that no one really looked forward to, but we all enjoyed it once we'd got started. Being nipped by the crabs is just as much a part of the lasting memory as appreciating the warm house afterwards!

Running the restaurant has its own challenges, but it has been very rewarding. We've made friends for life, whether it's past employees or regular customers, who we are still in touch with. It also allows us to live where we do, and for that I am grateful. We are lucky enough (on the odd occasion) to spot orcas and dolphins from our tables, and on a quiet summer's day, for me, there is no better place.

SMOKED MACKEREL ON TOAST WITH TOMATOES AND BALSAMIC VINEGAR

· ·

This is such a quick and easy lunch or dinner
that was very popular when we had it on the menu.

Splash of olive oil

Black pepper

Salt

8 cherry tomatoes

1 fillet of smoked mackerel

1 tbsp balsamic vinegar

Sourdough bread, toasted

Handful of coriander leaves

Heat up the olive oil in a small frying pan. Add a couple twists of black pepper and salt with the cherry tomatoes. Cook until the tomatoes are soft and slightly browned.

Break up the smoked mackerel into medium-size flakes. Once the tomatoes have softened and gently cooked, add the smoked mackerel and cook until the mackerel is hot throughout.

Add the balsamic vinegar to the pan and heat for a couple of minutes until the vinegar has cooked off, stirring to combine everything.

Serve the mackerel and tomato mixture on the toasted sourdough, topped with the fresh coriander.

PREPARATION TIME: 5 MINUTES | COOKING TIME: 10-15 MINUTES | SERVES 1-2

SISTA SHUCK!

BY KHATICHE AND REBEKAH LARCOMBE

"While women have always been an integral part of the fishing industry, our roles are often less visible and there are barriers that are difficult to overcome. Thankfully, things are changing, with more and more women involved at every level of the supply chain."

Growing up in a small former fishing town on the South Devon coast, we spent our childhood playing on beaches, in rivers, and at Brixham Harbour, an iconic maritime location steeped in fishing industry heritage. Brixham is one of the UK's oldest and busiest fishing ports with over 100 boats landing and selling their catch in the harbour. The mackerel, turbot, scallops, and crab – to name but a few – are some of the best in the world.

Despite this early introduction to the natural abundance of the ocean, we didn't eat any seafood until travelling and living abroad in our twenties. Unfortunately, other than the fantastic fish and chip shops and the occasional seafront stall selling pickled cockles and boiled prawns, access to local ocean produce was limited in our coastal towns in the nineties and early 2000s. Thankfully, much has since changed!

In October 2019, while living in London, we got into the fishmonger trade and have been seafood obsessed ever since. Through working in street food at Borough Market for many years, we had the opportunity to learn how to prepare a huge variety of fish and seafood. Starting with the basics of gutting fish and shucking oysters, we went on to learn how to fillet, butterfly, kipper and canoe. We've since cut and shucked all over London, forging relationships with some of the best boats, suppliers and artisan producers in the industry.

Fishmongery is, unfortunately, still overwhelmingly male dominated. While women have always been an integral part of the fishing industry, our roles are often less visible and there are barriers that are difficult to overcome. With such long hours and early starts, childcare is an issue for many. Thankfully, things are changing, with more and more women involved at every level of the supply chain. We love being a part of that movement!

The UK has some of the best ocean produce in the world, and we're passionate about championing the myriad fisherfolk and producers that supply it. Lately, we've been focusing on bivalves due to their amazing health benefits and unrivalled sustainability; we believe they are the food of the future and we should all be eating more of them. Having recently set up our own oyster shucking business, Sista Shuck!, our aim is to provide affordable luxury and highlight their miraculous health and environmental benefits to as many people as possible.

SMOKY PRESERVED SEAFOOD CHOWDER

Buying, storing and cooking live bivalves can be daunting, particularly for beginners! Smoked, pickled, cooked, and frozen bivalve meat is a great alternative, available from most seafood suppliers and supermarkets. This hearty preserved seafood chowder is a delicious, accessible way of incorporating seafood into your diet.

100g carrot

100g onion

100g leek

100g celery

400g waxy potatoes

50g butter

Glug of olive oil

Salt and pepper

2 fat cloves of garlic

125ml white wine (optional)

2 heaped tbsp plain flour

600ml fish stock (veg or chicken work too)

1 large bay leaf

60g pickled cockles

60g clams in brine

60g smoked oysters

60g smoked mussels

400ml single cream

Fresh parsley

Peel the carrot and onion. Rinse the leek and celery well to remove any grit. Chop all the vegetables into a medium dice. Chop the potatoes into small cubes of about half an inch (peel them first if preferred). Set aside.

Melt the butter with a dash of olive oil in a large saucepan on a medium heat. Add the carrot, onion, leek, and celery and season well with salt and pepper. Sauté on a medium heat, stirring occasionally, for 5 minutes, until softened but not browned.

While the veg sautés, peel and chop the garlic. Add to the pan and stir well. After 2 minutes, add the wine. Stir again and let the wine cook off for 1 minute.

Add the flour and stir well, making sure everything is coated. Turn the heat to low and cook the mixture for 2 minutes, stirring regularly.

Add a quarter of the stock and stir vigorously to avoid lumps. Turn the heat up to medium-high. Add the rest of the stock gradually, stirring continuously. Bring to a boil, then add the potatoes and bay leaf. Cover and simmer on a low heat for 10-12 minutes until the potatoes are tender, stirring occasionally.

Meanwhile, drain the cockles and clams. Drain and roughly chop the smoked oysters and mussels. All the smokiness comes from these, not bacon, in this chowder so be sure to include some. Leave a few whole if you like the texture or chop very fine if you don't! You can add or reduce the type and quantity of bivalve according to your own taste.

When the potatoes are tender, add the cream, stir well and simmer uncovered for 5 minutes on a medium low heat.

Add the seafood to the chowder and stir well. Remove pan from the heat. Let the chowder sit, lid on, for 5 minutes to allow the bivalves to warm through.

Chop the parsley and taste the chowder to check the seasoning. Add more salt and pepper if necessary. Chilli flakes are nice too! Garnish with the fresh parsley, add a wedge of lemon, and serve with crusty bread.

This also makes an excellent pie filling! Simply put the creamy mix into an oven dish, top with a sheet of pastry and bake at 180°c until golden brown. Puff is best, but filo and shortcrust work too.

PREPARATION TIME: 15 MINUTES | COOKING TIME: 30 MINUTES | SERVES 4

SOLE OF DISCRETION

BY CAROLINE BENNETT

"Sole of Discretion was born out of a desire to make it easier for the conscientious shopper to eat fish without that nagging doubt they might be contributing to a depleted and damaged marine ecosystem."

It is nigh impossible for most people to be able to differentiate fish that have been caught with minimal impact to the marine eco system and those that have wreaked considerable damage. Our mission is to make that easier. I'd been working on marine issues for two decades and being a pragmatist, it troubled me that there was no bridge between the well intentioned and highly knowledgeable environmental NGO community and people who wanted to do the right thing. Plenty of my friends would ask me what fish to eat and where to buy it, and there really were no easy answers. The only thing I could tell them was to look out for MSC (Marine Stewardship Council) species in the absence of any other clear guidelines, which was frustrating, as I knew there were far better fisheries out there.

Sole of Discretion was born out of a desire to make it easier for the conscientious shopper to eat fish without that nagging doubt they might be contributing to a depleted and damaged marine ecosystem. Everyone knows that to limit damage on the seas, hand-line-caught fish are some of the best, while it doesn't get much worse than dynamite (outlawed and yet still practiced in some parts of the world) but what about the rest? The vast majority of fishing lies somewhere in the middle of these two extremes. In this 99% grey area, there are some practices that are significantly better than others, and Sole of Discretion's aim is to help you navigate your way through. In a perfect world, perhaps we would return to anglers catching all our fish with a rod and line, but hand-line-caught fish will satisfy only a fraction of demand so becomes elitist, amplifies fishing pressure on a limited number of species, and just as importantly, does nothing to differentiate between the most damaging fisheries and many of the better small-scale ones.

If small-scale fishing is not differentiated from industrial, consumers are not able to actively support low-impact fishing, despite more and more people actively choosing to buy 'local' or 'ethical' and taking an interest in where their fish comes from as a result of rising awareness of the degradation of our seas. To help consumers chose, we are unique in the UK in that we offer full traceability back to the boat on each and every pack, telling our customers how their fish were caught. We are also the only fishmonger with a Soil Association approved manifesto.

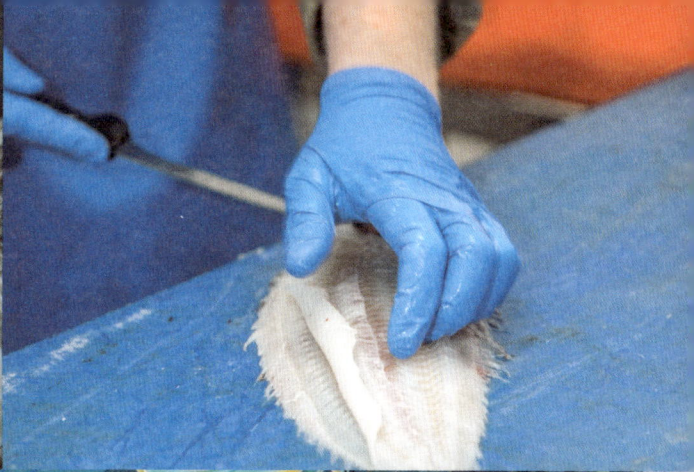

SKATE WING

· ·

Skate is an underutilised species and widely caught in the UK. If you are unable to get hold of capers, you can use chopped green olives as an alternative.

I ray wing fillet (about 400g)

100g plain flour (approximately, for dusting)

Salt and pepper

2 tbsp olive oil

250g salted butter

40g fresh dill or I tsp dried dill

I tbsp capers

½ lemon, zested and juiced

Have a dry, non-stick frying pan on a medium heat to warm while you prepare the ray wing fillet. Dust it lightly with flour on both sides and season with salt and pepper.

Add the oil to your warm pan and place the ray wing fillet in the pan, making sure that the thick middle part is lying flat. Fry for 4 minutes on each side, using a spatula and tongs to turn the fillet over. Do not be tempted to move the fish around the pan as the flesh will stick and tear.

Transfer the fillet to a baking tray and place into a preheated oven for 5 minutes at 180°c. Using the same pan you used to fry the fish, melt the butter along with the dill, capers, lemon zest and lemon juice. Cook on a medium heat for 5 minutes until the butter is a nutty brown colour.

Serve the brown butter sauce with the fish alongside a potato salad and a large glass of Pinot Grigio!

TEAM WILD WAVES

BY JESSICA OLIVER AND CHARLOTTE HARRIS, ATLANTIC ROWERS AND WORLD RECORD HOLDERS

"Our experience of training on the UK shores and then rowing the Atlantic Ocean was not only life-changing but a complete eye-opener. Being on the ocean for such a long period of time, outside in the elements, gave us such an appreciation for the magnitude of the sea and its wildlife."

In December 2021, we set off from La Gomera in the Canary Islands to row 3,000 miles across the Atlantic Ocean. After 45 days, we reached the shores of Antigua with a World Record as the fastest female pair to row the Atlantic, beating the previous record by five days. In the process, we raised £100,000 for Shelter and Women's Aid.

When we signed up to the challenge two years prior, neither of us had any ocean or rowing experience. Beach days and touristic boat trips were about as far as we got! We learnt how to row, navigate, weather route, and survive on the ocean. Our experience of training on the UK shores and then rowing the Atlantic Ocean was not only life-changing but a complete eye-opener. Being on the ocean for such a long period of time, outside in the elements, gave us such an appreciation for the magnitude of the sea and its wildlife.

During our crossing we saw sharks, dolphins, turtles and so much more. We battled huge storms. Our boat, Cosimo, capsized, we crashed into a fishing boat and sustained injuries from rowing 12-18 hours a day for over 45 days.

Over the two years leading up to the challenge and during the row itself, we relied on each other and our ten years of friendship. Monotonous days of rowing, feeling like we would never reach the other side, were filled with fun and laughter as we kept our spirts high. Never underestimate the power of a good team!

During the row we lived on dehydrated ration packs full of grains and beans. We dreamt of fresh ingredients; our first meal on land was a big salad full of vegetables and fruit. Our recipe is inspired not only by the ocean, but by the foods we ate and dreamt about during our crossing. We also used to prepare this recipe after long weekends training on the water. It's the dish of our friendship and something we always look forward to making together.

The ocean is a special place but is under threat. Be conscious of how you source your ingredients and protect our oceans and planet.

SEABASS WITH STUFFED PEPPERS AND COUSCOUS

We used to prepare this dish after long weekends training on the water in our ocean rowing boat. It's so simple to make and the perfect combination of healthy and comfort food. Couscous was also a staple on the Atlantic, so this recipe reminds us of our whole adventure.

1 red pepper

10 cherry tomatoes, halved

2 cloves of garlic, thinly sliced

2 anchovies, chopped

Olive oil

Salt and pepper

2 boneless sea bass fillets (skin on)

Butter

200g couscous

1 lemon

Handful of peas

Handful of broad beans

Handful of fresh mint

Handful of fresh flat leaf parsley

For the stuffed red pepper

Preheat the oven to 160°c/140°c fan/Gas Mark 3. Halve and deseed the red pepper, then place in a baking dish with the cut sides facing upwards.

Fill each red pepper half with 5 cherry tomatoes (10 halves), 1 sliced clove of garlic and 1 chopped anchovy. Drizzle with olive oil, season with salt and pepper, then roast in the preheated oven for 50 minutes until the tomatoes are soft and the peppers are filled with pools of tasty juice.

For the seabass

Pat the seabass fillets dry with kitchen paper, then dust with salt and pepper. Melt a generous knob of butter until bubbling in a wide pan and then place the seabass skin side down. Cook for 3 minutes on each side until the skin is crispy.

For the couscous

Cook the couscous as per the instructions on the packet, then add a good drizzle of olive oil and fresh lemon juice, separating the grains with a fork.

Meanwhile, cook the peas and broad beans in boiling water. Drain and then add to the couscous. Chop the fresh herbs and stir them through to finish.

To serve

Keep it simple! Place the couscous on the plate and lay the seabass on top, skin side up. Transfer the stuffed red pepper next to the couscous and seabass. The juices from the stuffed pepper make the perfect sauce. Enjoy!

PREPARATION TIME: 20 MINUTES | COOKING TIME: 50 MINUTES | SERVES 2

TRINITY HOUSE

BY JAMIE CAMPBELL AND ALICE PROUT

"We are very lucky to be working at sea, surrounded by some of the best seafood in the world, from beautiful Cromer crabs and lobster from the northeast to the freshest line-caught mackerel in the southwest; there's nothing better than lighting the barbecue and cooking fresh mackerel while watching the sun go down."

As shipping lanes around the UK grow increasingly crowded and our demand for consumer goods rises, the safe transit of ships and seafarers is more important than ever. As part of the maritime sector's vital works to ensure that seafarers make safe passage and for supermarket and high street shelves to remain stocked, Trinity House provides over 600 aids to navigation – such as lighthouses, buoys, lightvessels and beacons – in its capacity as the General Lighthouse Authority for England, Wales, the Channel Islands and Gibraltar.

Our aids to navigation help thousands of mariners annually to navigate their way safely around some of the UK's busiest waters including the Dover Strait, the world's busiest shipping lane. Continuing the same thread of work that started in 1514, Trinity House's fleet of three vessels carry out marine operations in our waters and are an instantly recognisable mainstay of the British coastline. THV Patricia has just celebrated her 40th year in service and – along with her sisters THVs Galatea and Alert – continues to keep the busy sea ways around Dover clear for safe passage around the coast of England and Wales.

On any given day, scheduled work could include buoy maintenance, transfer of staff to offshore lighthouses by helicopter or boat, lightvessel towing or locating, and marking wrecks and other marine hazards. THV Patricia has a crew of 21 on each of its 'Port' and 'Starboard' watches, each serving three weeks on followed by three weeks off. Each watch has a complement of well-trained and qualified officers and crew on the bridge, in the engine room and on deck; all depend on good catering to make the ship feel like their home from home for those three weeks.

Catering Manager Jamie Campbell has served with Trinity House for over 28 years, starting as a trainee before earning promotions through the ranks of 2nd Cook and Chief Cook. Alice Prout also started at Trinity House as a trainee, then went on to earn a position as Chief Cook and has been in post for ten years. We are very lucky to be working at sea, surrounded by some of the best seafood in the world, from beautiful Cromer crabs and lobster from the northeast to the freshest line caught mackerel in the southwest. There's nothing better than lighting the barbecue and cooking fresh mackerel while watching the sun go down.

CHILLI AND LIME GRIDDLED SWORDFISH WITH FRESH SALSA

· ·

The delicious lime and chilli marinade in this recipe works with other fish as well. If you are using fish fillets with skin, use a frying pan instead of a griddle and place the fish skin side down first to get it nice and crispy.

I red chilli

2 cloves of garlic

I lime, zested and juiced

I-2 tbsp olive oil

4 swordfish fillets, 150-200g each

For the salsa

2 tomatoes

¼ cucumber

I red onion

I pepper (red, yellow or orange)

I red chilli, deseeded

I clove of garlic

Handful of fresh coriander

I lime, zested and juice

2 tsp olive oil

I tsp red wine vinegar

Sea salt and cracked black pepper, to taste

Finely chop the chilli (you can keep the seeds in if you like more heat) and garlic, then mix these with the lime zest, lime juice, and olive oil. Spread the mixture over the swordfish fillets and leave to marinate for 40 minutes to I hour.

For the salsa

Dice the tomatoes, cucumber, onion and pepper, then place them in a bowl. Finely chop the chilli, garlic and coriander, then add them to the diced ingredients. Combine the lime zest and juice with the oil and vinegar, then pour this dressing into the bowl. Toss the salsa to coat everything evenly, then season with a little sea salt and cracked black pepper to taste.

To cook and serve

Heat a griddle pan until almost smoking. Place the marinated swordfish in the hot pan and cook for 2-3 minutes on one side. Once the fillets have nice griddle marks on the underside, turn them over and cook for a further 5 minutes.

We like to serve the swordfish and salsa with pan-fried sliced new potatoes and sprouting broccoli with sesame seeds.

PREPARATION TIME: 15 MINUTES, PLUS MARINATING | COOKING TIME: 10 MINUTES | SERVES 4

TWO BROTHERS FISHING

BY SARAH READY

"If you want a future in this industry, it's in your interest to do everything you can to ensure the stocks are there for next year – I don't know anyone who doesn't fish sustainably to look after their 'patch'."

I've always been entrenched within the fishing industry as part of my husband's career as a trawlerman and trawler owner in South Devon. I began as a lawyer and very quickly, fishermen started coming to me for help with their paperwork. Now, most of my time is spent running a law clinic where they can come for free advice; we've got about 27 solicitors and barristers who work pro bono alongside me to support fishermen. I'm passionate about this because the fishing industry is finding it harder and harder to keep going under all the regulatory burdens since we've come out of Brexit, with both EU and UK legislation that is very difficult for fishermen to navigate.

Within the family business, my husband and I have gradually moved towards more sustainable fishing practices. We use a zero-plastic potting system on our very small potting open day boat; I've been researching willow potting, the traditional fishing method for catching crab and lobster, and its heritage for about ten years now and making pots myself for about five or six years. In 2022 I was lucky enough to receive a small bursary from the Queen Elizabeth Scholarship Trust to boost this endangered craft and enable me to continue learning the technique from Dave French, a fifth generation withy pot maker.

We've also been chosen to build the first electric fishing boat through the Seafood Innovation Fund, who assess projects like ours to determine their scientific and environmental benefits. So far, we have scaled up to buying a catamaran with electric outboards and lithium batteries to see whether we can get out to the fishing grounds with a purely electric boat for netting as well as potting. If you want a future in this industry, it's in your interest to do everything you can to ensure the stocks are there for next year – I don't know anyone who doesn't fish sustainably to look after their 'patch'.

Currently 100% of our trawled fish goes to a fish market and probably 90% of that goes to Europe – I'm more likely to eat fish we've caught in Portugal or Spain than here in Brixham. However, Rockfish takes our catch from the willow pots for its restaurants, meaning we don't even have to get in the car to deliver our produce from where it's landed, just how it should be. It's a shame that the British consumer doesn't really support fishermen as far as buying their produce goes; I think we need a cultural shift towards eating more fish from our native waters for a truly sustainable future.

Welcome to Brixham Marina

SQUID STUFFED WITH
HERBY SMOKED AND WHITE FISH
· ·

In this recipe, calamari tubes are stuffed with seasonal, locally sourced white fish and smoked fish, before being cooked just like sausages. The calamari sausages are very versatile and can be eaten on their own, served with a salad or potatoes, or baked in a cheese sauce.

4 small to medium squid, cleaned

500g white and smoked fish, cooked (a fish pie mixture is good for this recipe)

2 tbsp roughly chopped flat leaf parsley

2 tbsp roughly chopped basil

2 tbsp chopped chives

2 tbsp grated parmesan

1 lemon, zested

1 tbsp extra virgin olive oil

Salt and pepper

Cherry tomatoes (optional)

Dry the squid and roughly chop the tentacles. For the stuffing, place the cooked fish, chopped herbs, parmesan, lemon zest, tentacles and olive oil in a bowl. Mix until combined, then season to taste.

Stuff the cleaned and dried squid, closing the ends with toothpicks. Chill until ready to cook.

Put a heavy griddle pan on the hob over a high heat. Place the stuffed squid in the pan and cook for around 15 minutes or until slightly brown on the outside, turning as they cook. Be careful not to burn the calamari.

If desired, cherry tomatoes can be added to the pan towards the end of the cooking time. This works well if you're eating the stuffed squid with potatoes and cooked vegetables. Alternatively, simply serve them with a fresh salad for a lighter summery meal.

Tips: The amount of filling does not have to be an exact science as the result will be the same, as long as the stuffed squid are packed down and left to chill before cooking in a griddle pan.

PREPARATION TIME: 20 MINUTES | COOKING TIME: 20 MINUTES | SERVES 2 HUNGRY PEOPLE, OR FOUR AS A LIGHT SUPPER

DIRECTORY

· ·

A&J Fresh Fish Ltd
Address: 20 North Scale, Walney Island,
Barrow-in-Furness, Cumbria, LA14 3RW
Facebook: A&J Fresh Fish Ltd
Instagram @ajfreshfishltd

*We are a small business based on Walney Island, supplying
sustainable fish and shellfish which is all caught by us from our
own boat.*

Barneys Billingsgate Limited
Address: Shop 1, Unit Q6/7, Billingsgate Market,
Trafalgar Way, London E14 5ST
Telephone: 02074 812177
Website: Barneys-seafood.co.uk
Email: barneysseafood@gmail.com
Instagram @barneysseafood
Twitter @TheJelliedeel

*We supply wholesale jellied eels, shellfish and fish. We are a
family-run business with family values. We pride ourselves on our
customer services.*

CHADFISH
Address: 34 Gordon Road, Topsham, Exeter EX3 0LJ
Telephone: 07307 863233
Email: chadfish@hotmail.co.uk
Twitter @andychadwick63

Supplier of smoked fish.

Coastal Foraging
Address: 10 Plasgwyn Road, Penygroes,
Llanelli, Carmarthenshire, SA14 7RY
Telephone: 07989 143868
Website: www.coastalforaging.co.uk
Email: info@coastalforaging.co.uk
Instagram @Coastal_Foraging_with_Craig
Facebook and YouTube: Coastal Foraging with Craig Evans

*Professional and fun coastal foraging courses and much more.
We cook and eat what we find on the beach in the beautifully
diverse coastline of South West Wales.*

Cornish Sea Salt
Address: Lower Quay, Gweek, Helston, TR12 6UD
Telephone: 01326 554720
Website: www.cornishseasalt.co.uk
Email: info@cornishseasalt.co.uk
Find us on Instagram | Facebook | LinkedIn | Twitter | TikTok

*Cornish Sea Salt is harvested fresh from Cornish waters, just
eight metres from our eco-friendly Salt House, and is packed with
over 60 unique minerals to add maximum flavour to cooking.*

Crabpotcellars
Address: Kittiwake, Bolberry Road, Inner Hope,
nr Kingsbridge, South Devon TQ7 3HT
Telephone: 01548 560237
Email: crabpotcellars@hotmail.com
Facebook and Instagram: Susan Morgan

*I am a basketmaker, specialising in withy crabpots, married
to a local crab fisherman. I also make other baskets and am
interested in their social history and functional forms.*

Crabby Skipper
Address: Laura N162 Fishing Boat c/o Kilkeel Harbour
Email: crabbyskipper162@outlook.com
Twitter @CrabbySkipper
Instagram @crabbyskipper162

*Family fishing boat specialising in sustainable seasonal shellfish
including lobsters, brown crab and velvet crab. Our shellfish is
sold to a local family-operated shellfish processor in Kilkeel, from
where it can be shipped all over the world.*

Dai's Shed
Address: The Wharf, Canolfan Dyfi, Aberdyfi LL35 0EE
Telephone: 07944 264 821 (during the fishing season only)
Email: gill@gillyfish.co.uk

*A local fisherman catching and selling fish and shellfish including
lobster, crab, prawns and whelks caught off the Aberdyfi coast.*

Dan The Fish Man

Telephone: 07970 932566
Email: dan@clovellyfish.co.uk
Facebook @clovellyfish
Twitter @ClovellyfishDan
Instagram @dan_thefishman
TikTok @danclovellyfish
YouTube: Dan The Fish Man

I encourage people to experience the very best in fish and seafood cooking through buying and selling local fish, visiting schools to cook simple healthy recipes, and other social initiatives in my beautifully North Devon village of Clovelly.

David C. Morgan

Address: Kittiwake, Bolberry Road, Inner Hope,
nr Kingsbridge, South Devon TQ7 3HT
Telephone: 01548 560237
Email: morgan_dc@hotmail.com
Social Media: South Devon and Channel Shellfishermen Ltd

I fish from my own 10 metre inshore boat, the Southern Star, out of Salcombe along the South Devon coast. The catch is brown crab and lobster, with occasional netting for wetfish.

Dorset Shellfish Ltd

Address: Unit 4, Maritime Business Centre,
Portland, Dorset, DT5 1FD
Telephone: 07881 632311
Website: www.dorset-shellfish.co.uk
Email: info@dorset-shellfish.com
Facebook and Instagram @dorsetshellfish

We are a fishing family from Weymouth. We sell crab, lobster and line-caught fish direct to the public. Our crab meat is handpicked and made into dressed crabs, crab cakes and lots more.

Ewing Seafoods

Address: 6 Kendal Street, Belfast, BT13 2JR Northern Ireland
Telephone: 028 9032 5534
Email: sales@ewingseafoods.co.uk
Facebook, Instagram and Twitter @ewingseafoods

Belfast based fishmongers supplying fresh local fish and seafood to Northern Ireland's top restaurants and hotels.

Fish City

Address: 33 Ann Street, Belfast BT1 4EB, Northern Ireland
Telephone: 028 9023 1000
Website: www.fish-city.com
Email: events@fish-city.com
Social Media @fishcitybelfast

Fish City is an award-winning, family-owned seafood and fish & chip restaurant in the heart of Belfast City Centre serving fresh, local and sustainable fish and seafood.

Fishing into the Future

Address: Fishmongers' Hall, London Bridge,
London EC4R 9EL
Telephone: 07311 812105
Website: www.fishingporthole.co.uk
/ www.fishingintothefuture.co.uk (we also highly rate visiting www.discoverseafood.uk)
Email: emma@fitf.co.uk
LinkedIn: Fishing into the Future
Facebook @fishingintothefuture
Instagram @fishing_porthole
Twitter @fishing_future

UK charity run by fishermen, for fishermen. Sharing knowledge, developing skills, and creating connections between fishermen, people in the seafood industry, science, and management.

The Fish Works

Address: 3 The Promenade, Largs, KA30 8BG
Telephone: 01475 674111
Website: www.thefishworks.co.uk
Email: hello@thefishworks.co.uk
Facebook and Twitter @fishworkslargs
Instagram @thefishworks

The Fish Works is a family business run by The Irvins. They wanted to create somewhere in Largs to enjoy fresh quality Scottish seafood with the best views of the Firth of Clyde.

Food Teachers Centre Community (Fish Hero Programme)

Address: Clarkson Hyde, 3rd Floor Chancery House, St Nicholas Way, Sutton, Surrey SM1 1JB
Website: www.foodteacherscentre.co.uk
Email: info@footeacherscentre.co.uk
Social Media @FoodTCentre @fish.heroes

The Food Teachers Centre is an online community of secondary school Food, Nutrition and Catering teachers, working in partnership with industry supporters to provide training, teaching resources and advice to teachers across the UK.

The Girlyfishmonger

Facebook: The Girlyfishmonger
Twitter @girlyfishmonger
Instagram @girlyfishmonger1983

Emma McKeating is an Advanced Fishmonger on the Master Fishmonger Standard, passionate about her industry and sharing knowledge with others.

Frazers Scallops – The Handpicked Scallops Company LTD

Address: Beardon Farm, Higher Ashton, Exeter, EX6 7QT
Telephone: 07742 601354
Email: frazersscallops@gmail.com
Facebook: The Handpicked Scallop Company
Instagram @frazersscallops

Regenerative fishing by means of diving: zero bycatch, zero destruction. We are a small team of scallop divers, passionate about the ocean and working with Mother Nature, supplying hand dived scallops to the best chefs in the country and the public.

Inka Cresswell

Address: 22 Thornhill Crescent, Islington, London
Telephone: 07711 979570
Website: www.inkacresswell.com
Email: inka-liberty@hotmail.co.uk
Social Media @inkacresswell

Inka Cresswell is a freelance wildlife filmmaker and underwater photographer who specialises in telling stories about our wild blue spaces. She uses her camera to educate the public about marine conservation and hopes her work will educate and inspire a new generation of conservationists.

Isla Gale

Telephone: 07624 273173
Email: isla.gale@galeforce10.co.uk

Female fisherman fishing scallops and queenies.

Island Fish Ltd.

Address: Island Fish, Kenython, Bryher, Isles of Scilly, TR230PR
Telephone: 01720 423880
Website: www.islandfish.co.uk
Email: contactus@islandfish.co.uk
Twitter @IOSfish

Suppliers of high quality fish and shellfish to the Isles of Scilly for as far back as we can trace!

Jade-S Fisheries Jersey

Address: Jade-S Fisheries, Unit V12M, Victoria Pier, St Helier, Jersey, Channel Islands, JE2 3NB
Telephone: 077977 45018
Website: www.jadesfisheries.com
Email: jadesfisheriesjersey@gmail.com
Facebook and Instagram @jadesfisheriesjersey
Twitter @jadesfisheries
LinkedIn: Jade-S Fisheries Jersey

Jade-S Fisheries is a family fishing and fish merchant business in Jersey CI, run by partners in life and business Captain Leyton Hunnisett and his 'first mate' Gabby Mason.

Jersey Seafaris

Address: St Catherine's Breakwater, St Martins, Jersey
Telephone: 07829 772222
Website: www.jerseyseafaris.com
Email: info@jerseyseafaris.com
Social Media @Jersey Seafaris

Jersey Seafaris is the ultimate Jersey experience! From an exhilarating RIB ride to a lobster picnic and glass of champagne on a deserted beach, dolphin spotting, or even zipping across to France for dinner, there is a Seafari for everyone.

Johnsons Enterprises Ltd

Address: Unit 4, Portsmouth Food Centre,
Norway Road, PO3 5HT Portsmouth
Telephone: 02392 817547
Website: www.johnsonsfish.com
Email: info@johnsonsenterprises.com
Facebook: Johnsons Enterprises
Instagram @johnsonsfish1

Providing quality fresh and frozen fish and shellfish to the trade and public since 1975. Visiting various farm shops across Hampshire & West Sussex and bringing local produce to you.

Marine Conservation Society

Address: Overross House, Ross Park,
Ross-on-Wye, HR9 7US
Telephone: 01989 566017
Website: www.mcsuk.org
Email: info@mcsuk.org
Facebook and Twitter @mcsuk
Instagram @mcs_uk

The Marine Conservation Society fights for the future of our ocean through people-powered action, with science on our side. For seas full of life, where nature flourishes and people thrive.

Ninth Wave Restaurant

Address: Bruach Mhor, Fionnphort, Mull, PA66 6BL
Telephone: 01681 700757
Website: www.ninthwaverestaurant.co.uk
Email: enquiries@ninthwaverestaurant.co.uk

A wee gem of a seafood restaurant on the Hebridean Isle of Mull, specialising in luxury four course group lunches.

Offshore Shellfish Ltd.

Telephone: 07736045150
Website: www.offshoreshellfish.com
Email: sarah@offshoreshellfish.com
Facebook and Instagram @offshoreshellfish
Twitter @offshoreshell
LinkedIn: Offshore Shellfish

Offshore Shellfish is a family-run mussel farming business based in South Devon, growing premium quality, sustainable rope grown mussels in the offshore waters of the Atlantic in Lyme Bay.

Orkney Fisheries Association

Address: OA Building, Kirkwall Pier, Kirkwall,
Orkney, KW15 1LG
Telephone: 01856 871818
Website: www.orkneyfisheries.com
Email: info@orkneyfisheries.com
Social Media @orkneyfisheries

Orkney Fisheries Association is a trade body representing the interests of Orkney's fishing fleet. OFA works closely with fishermen, scientists and other fishing organisations to represent the interests of Orkney's fishing industry, promote sustainable fishing practices and to help improve the knowledge of the marine environment and the species within it.

Osborne & Sons (Shellfish) Limited

Address: Nos. 7-9 The Cocklesheds, High Street,
Leigh-on-Sea, Essex, SS9 2ER
Telephone: 01702 477387
Website: www.osbornes.fish
Email: hello@osbornes.fish
Social Media @osbornesfish

Cockle and whelk processor, fishmonger, seafood café and kitchen, seafood training school. Situated in the heart of Old Leigh, a fifth generation family-run business.

Padstow Boatyard

Address: South Quay, Padstow, PL28 8BL
Telephone: 01841 533674
Website: www.padstow-boatyard.com
Email: jon@padstow-boatyard.com
Facebook: Padstow Boatyard
Instagram @padstow_boatyard

Padstow Boatyard are experienced commercial fishing boat builders, offering build, repair and refit services to the UK fishing fleet from the heart of Padstow, Cornwall.

Rockfish

Website: www.therockfish.co.uk
Social Media @therockfishuk

At Rockfish we are on a mission to change the way you experience seafood. Enjoy fresh local seafood at our coastal restaurants across Devon and Dorset or delivered to your door from our online seafood market.

Rossmore Oysters Ltd.

Address: Lakeview, Old Hollow, Worth,
West Sussex, RH10 4TA
Telephone: 01293 888868
Website: www.oysters.co.uk
Email: tristan@oysters.co.uk

Oyster farmer and breeder of the finest oysters from around our shores, from England, Ireland, Scotland, but not yet Wales!

Scott's Richmond

Address: 4 Whittaker Avenue, Richmond, TW9 1EH
Telephone: 0207 6476325
Website: www.scotts-richmond.com
Email: tfraser@scotts-restaurant.com
Instagram @cheftomfraser

Seafood restaurant and oyster bar, located on the river in Richmond.

Sea Haze

Address: 207 Kings Road Arches, Brighton Seafront
Telephone: 01273 777007
Website: www.seahazefreshfish.co.uk
Email: info@seahazefreshfish.co.uk
Facebook: Sea Haze Fresh Fish Shop
Instagram @sea_haze_seafoods

Sea Haze is a family-run business that has been supporting Brighton seafront for the last 30 years with fresh produce sourced from our family-run fishing boat.

Sea Marie

Website: www.seamarie.co.uk / www.mariebuchanan.com
Email: marie@seamarie.co.uk
Instagram @mariebuchanan

Sea Marie offers coaching, fitness and physiotherapy specialising in injury rehabilitation and prevention for water sports and outdoor lovers including runners, paddlers, surfers and water-based wind sports.

The Shorehouse Seafood Restaurant

Address: Tigh na mara, Tarbet, Scourie, Lairg,
Sutherland, IV27 4SS
Telephone: 01971 502251
Website: www.shorehousetarbet.co.uk
Facebook: Shorehouse Seafood Restaurant

Small, seasonal family-run seafood restaurant. Our own boat supplies all our shellfish.

Sista Shuck!

Address: The Bird's Nest, 32 Deptford Church Street,
Lewisham, London, SE8 4RZ plus roaming pop-ups!
Website: www.sistashuck.com
Email: sistashuck@gmail.com
Social Media @twinseatworld

We source our oysters from small, sustainable aquaculture farms across the UK, shucking and serving them up raw, fried or grilled. Everyone welcome. Luxury for all!

Sole of Discretion

Address: 5 Fish Quay, Sutton Harbour, Plymouth, PL4 0LH

Telephone: 01752 657528

Website: www.soleofdiscretion.co.uk

Email: us@soleofdiscretion.co.uk

Instagram @sole_of_discretion

Twitter @SoDiscretion

Facebook: SoleofDiscretion

Sole of Discretion are committed to procuring fish and shellfish that have been caught with as little damage to the marine environment as possible.

Team Wild Waves (Ocean Rowers)

Address: 16 Emu Road, SW8 3PR

Telephone: 07811372830

Website: www.teamwildwaves.com

Email: jessicamoliver@hotmail.co.uk

Social Media @teamwildwaves @jessica.maeve.oliver @charley.harris

Best friends, ocean rowers, world record holders.

Traditional Lobster Pots and Two Brothers Fishing Limited

Address: 51 Berry Head Road, Brixham, Devon, TQ5 9AA

Telephone: 07402 089170

Website: www.traditionallobsterpots.co.uk

Email: sarah@traditionallobsterpots.co.uk

Twitter @fishsarah

Instagram @girlyfisherman

Family fishing business in Brixham, South Devon. I am a female fisherman and traditional lobster pot maker, working with and preserving the heritage of traditional withy pots.

Trinity House

Address: Trinity House, Tower Hill, London, EC3N 4DH

Telephone: 020 7481 6900

Website: www.trinityhouse.co.uk

Email: enquiries@trinityhouse.co.uk

Twitter @trinityhouse_uk

Instagram @trinityhouseuk @foodie_on_the_waves

Trinity House is a General Lighthouse Authority and maritime charity working for the benefit and safety of all mariners.

TITLES IN THIS SERIES

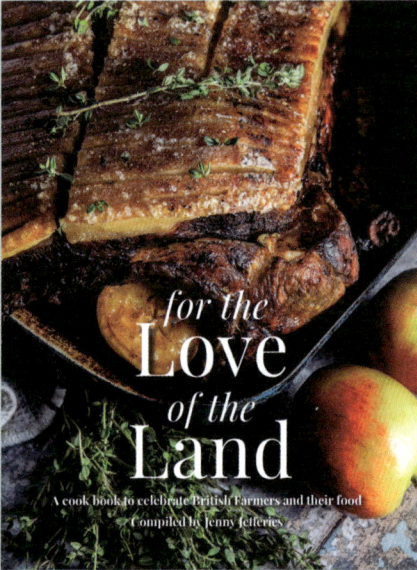

This is a cook book to celebrate British farming in all its hardship and glory. For many families, working the land and raising livestock is a true labour of love, and what they produce is the backbone of the country's food and drink. The dishes in this book make the most of local and seasonal ingredients, creating delicious meals, puddings and bakes that anyone can cook up at home. Alongside that, members of these farming families have told the stories of their livelihoods: from losing sheep in snowstorms to stoking enthusiasm in the next generation, their honesty and passion is an inspiration and an education. Recipes include Blackbrook Beef Bolognese from a traditional lowland farm in Leicestershire, Reestit Mutton Soup by two sisters who run their family farm on Shetland and Pheasant and Asparagus Crumble by game farmers from Cambridgeshire, as well as Kentish Lavender Shortbread from Castle Farm and a cocktail featuring fresh edible flowers from Greens of Devon. As the landscape of British farming changes, we need to support high-quality food production and understand how farmers can work in harmony with nature to make our eating habits more sustainable. Whether you're country born and bred or have never donned a pair of wellies, discover the food and stories in this book to help put British farming back on the map. 12% of Jenny's net profits from the sales of For The Love of the Land is being donated to the National Literacy Trust.

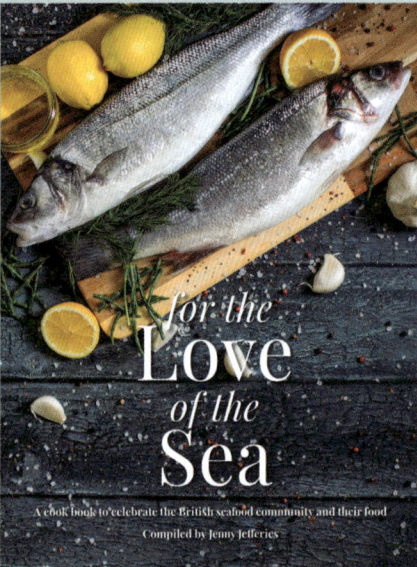

Following the success of For The Love of the Land, this second cook book compiled by Jenny Jefferies and produced by Meze Publishing showcases the incredible fish and seafood found in the UK. For The Love of the Sea highlights the hard work and dedication of the men and women who work in the British fishing industry, as well as those who support them such as the Royal National Lifeboat Institution. The book features professional sailors, fishmongers, fishermen and women, marine conservationists, chefs and suppliers, as well as a foreword by Marcus Coleman, the Chief Executive of Seafish which works with businesses and the government to support the UK seafood sector. With over 40 delicious recipes and fascinating stories from the contributors, For The Love of the Sea aims to encourage everyone to fall in love with British fish and seafood again, championing sustainability and celebrating great produce.

12% of Jenny's net profits from the sales of For The Love of the Sea is being donated to the RNLI.

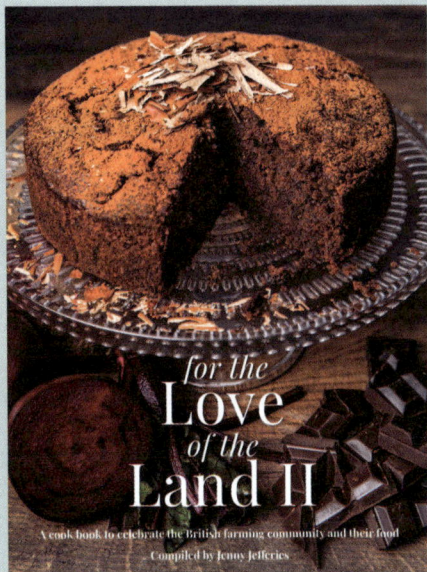

Celebrating our amazing farmers and the food they produce, this timely and topical sequel highlights 40 of the UK's most influential and innovative farms including Riverford, Yeo Valley, Belvoir and the Michelin-starred Cumbrian restaurant, L'Enclume. For The Love of the Land II features a delicious range of recipes, from British meats to knockout vegetarian dishes and irresistible desserts, as well as fascinating insights into cutting-edge farming practices that put conservation and sustainability at the forefront of our food production. Suitable for home cooks of any skill level, this book is also the perfect read for anyone who is interested in where their food comes from.

10% of Jenny's net profits from the sales of For The Love of the Land II is being donated to The Farm Safety Foundation aka Yellow Wellies.

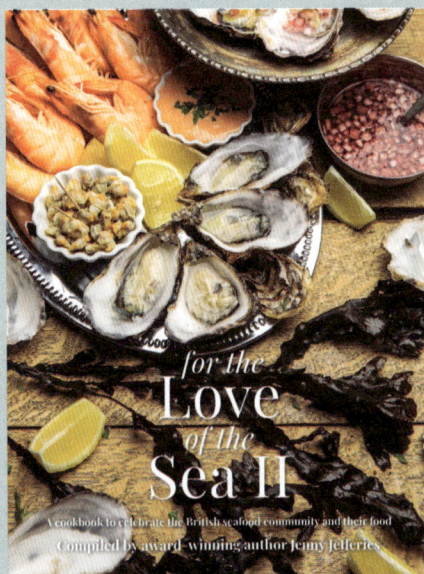

For The Love of the Sea II is a compilation by award-winning author Jenny Jefferies that celebrates Britain's cornucopian coastline through the people, produce and practices that define it. Discover the stories and recipes of 40 contributors, from fishmongers to foragers and basket weavers to marine scientists, or find your next destination restaurant to sample freshly caught seafood all over the UK. Home cooks will love the variety of delicious dishes to try: Haddock Scotch Egg, Thai Red Curry Mussels, Stargazy Pie and Mediterranean Roasted Whole Seabass are just a few of the recipes included. With 10% of the net profits going to The Food Teachers Centre charity, this book champions sustainability and education, helping us all to fall back in love with our shores.